INCOME INEQUALITY

AN ALARMING U.S. TREND

ECONOMIC ISSUES, PROBLEMS AND PERSPECTIVES

Additional books in this series can be found on Nova's website under the Series tab.

Additional E-books in this series can be found on Nova's website under the E-books tab.

AMERICA IN THE 21ST CENTURY: POLITICAL AND ECONOMIC ISSUES

Additional books in this series can be found on Nova's website under the Series tab.

Additional E-books in this series can be found on Nova's website under the E-books tab.

ECONOMIC ISSUES, PROBLEMS AND PERSPECTIVES

INCOME INEQUALITY

AN ALARMING U.S. TREND

Ruth D. Alford
and
Rod Reilly
EDITOR

Nova Science Publishers, Inc.
New York

NOTICE TO THE READER

The Publisher has taken reasonable care in the preparation of this book, but makes no expressed or implied warranty of any kind and assumes no responsibility for any errors or omissions. No liability is assumed for incidental or consequential damages in connection with or arising out of information contained in this book. The Publisher shall not be liable for any special, consequential, or exemplary damages resulting, in whole or in part, from the readers' use of, or reliance upon, this material. Any parts of this book based on government reports are so indicated and copyright is claimed for those parts to the extent applicable to compilations of such works.

Independent verification should be sought for any data, advice or recommendations contained in this book. In addition, no responsibility is assumed by the publisher for any injury and/or damage to persons or property arising from any methods, products, instructions, ideas or otherwise contained in this publication.

This publication is designed to provide accurate and authoritative information with regard to the subject matter covered herein. It is sold with the clear understanding that the Publisher is not engaged in rendering legal or any other professional services. If legal or any other expert assistance is required, the services of a competent person should be sought. FROM A DECLARATION OF PARTICIPANTS JOINTLY ADOPTED BY A COMMITTEE OF THE AMERICAN BAR ASSOCIATION AND A COMMITTEE OF PUBLISHERS.

Additional color graphics may be available in the e-book version of this book.

Library of Congress Cataloging-in-Publication Data

ISBN 978-1-61942-511-8

Published by Nova Science Publishers, Inc. † New York

CONTENTS

PREFACE

This book examines real (inflation-adjusted) average household income, from 1979 to 2007 (because those endpoints allow comparisons between periods of similar overall economic activity as they were both years before recessions). During that period, the evolution of the nation's economy and the tax and spending policies of the federal government and state and local governments had varying effects on households at different points in the income distribution. The share in income accruing to higher-income households increased, whereas the share accruing to other households declined. As a result of that uneven income growth, the distribution of after-tax household income in the U.S. was substantially more unequal in 2007 than in 1979.

Chapter 1- From 1979 to 2007, real (inflation-adjusted) average household income, measured after government transfers and federal taxes, grew by 62 percent. During that period, the evolution of the nation's economy and the tax and spending policies of the federal government and state and local governments had varying effects on households at different points in the income distribution: Income after transfers and federal taxes (denoted as after-tax income in this study) for households at the higher end of the income scale rose much more rapidly than income for households in the middle and at the lower end of the income scale.[1] In particular:

For the 1 percent of the population with the highest income, average real after-tax household income grew by 275 percent between 1979 and 2007 (see Summary Figure 1).

For others in the 20 percent of the population with the highest income (those in the 81st through 99th percentiles), average real after-tax household income grew by 65 percent over that period, much faster than it did for the remaining 80 percent of the population, but not nearly as fast as for the top 1 percent.

For the 60 percent of the population in the middle of the income scale (the 21st through 80th percentiles), the growth in average real after-tax household income was just under 40 percent.

For the 20 percent of the population with the lowest income, average real after-tax household income was about 18 percent higher in 2007 than it had been in 1979.

Chapter 2- Understanding how the annual earnings of workers have changed over time is integral to projecting possible changes in such earnings in the future and considering government tax and spending policies that affect workers. This Congressional Budget Office (CBO) paper documents changes in workers' annual earnings; however, it does not delve deeply into the causes of those changes or the possible implications for government policy.

The paper first describes changes between 1979 and 2007 in the annual (inflation-adjusted) earnings of workers ages 25 to 54. CBO found that men with relatively low, median, and relatively high earnings (specifically, men at the 10th, 50th, and 90th percentiles of their earnings distribution) earned more than women in the same position of their own earnings distribution in 2007, and that those differences were smaller in 2007 than in 1979 (see Figure 1). (Box 1 presents a primer on some of the measurement concepts used in this paper.) CBO also compared the differences in earnings between low, median, and high earners of the same sex in a given year. For men, the ratio of the earnings of high earners to those of median earners was larger in 2007 than in 1979, whereas the earnings ratio for median and low earners was roughly the same in the two years. For women, in contrast, the ratio of the earnings of high earners to those of median earners was roughly the same in 2007 as it was in 1979, but the earnings ratio for median and low earners was smaller in 2007 than it was in 1979.

In: Income Inequality
Eds: R. D. Alford and R. Reilly

ISBN: 978-1-61942-511-8
© 2012 Nova Science Publishers, Inc.

Chapter 1

TRENDS IN THE DISTRIBUTION OF HOUSEHOLD INCOME BETWEEN 1979 AND 2007[*]

Congressional Budget Office

NOTES AND DEFINITIONS

Numbers in the text, tables, and figures may not add up to totals because of rounding. Unless otherwise indicated, all years referred to in this study are calendar years.

Some of the figures have shaded vertical bars that indicate the duration of recessions. (A recession extends from the peak of a business cycle to its trough.)

Income is adjusted for inflation using the Bureau of Labor Statistics' research series of the consumer price index for all urban consumers (CPI-U-RS).

Income is adjusted for differences in household size—specifically, by dividing income by the square root of a household's size. (A household consists of the people who share a housing unit, regardless of their relationships.)

---

[*] This is an edited, reformatted and augmented version of a Congress of the United States Congressional Budget Office publication, dated October 2011.

Income categories are defined by ranking all households by their size-adjusted income. Percentiles (hundredths) and quintiles (fifths) contain equal numbers of people. Households with negative income are excluded from the lowest income category but are included in totals.

A household with children has at least one member under age 18. An elderly childless household is headed by a person age 65 or older with no member under age 18. A nonelderly childless household is one headed by a person under age 65 and with no member under age 18.

Market income includes the following components:

- Labor income, which includes cash wages and salaries (including those allocated by employees to 401(k) plans), employer-paid health insurance premiums, and the employer's share of Social Security, Medicare, and federal unemployment insurance payroll taxes.

- Business income, which includes net income from businesses and farms operated solely by their owners, partnership income, and income from S corporations.

- Capital gains, which are profits realized from the sale of assets. Increases in the value of assets that have not been realized through sales are not included in market income.

- Capital income (excluding capital gains) comprises taxable and tax-exempt interest, dividends paid by corporations (but not dividends from S corporations, which are considered part of business income), positive rental income, and corporate income taxes. Capital gains are considered separately and not included in this measure of capital income. The Congressional Budget Office assumes in this analysis that corporate income taxes are borne by owners of capital in proportion to their income from capital; therefore, the amount of the corporate tax is included in household income measured before taxes.

- Other income, which includes income received in retirement for past services and any other sources of income.

Transfer income includes cash payments from Social Security, unemployment insurance, Supplemental Security Income, Aid to Families with Dependent Children, Temporary Assistance for Needy Families, veterans' benefits, workers' compensation, and state and local government assistance programs, as well as the value of in-kind benefits, including food stamps, school lunches and breakfasts, housing assistance, energy assistance, Medicare, Medicaid, and the Children's Health Insurance Program (health benefits are measured as the fungible value, a Census Bureau estimate of the value to recipients).

After-tax income is equal to market income plus transfer income minus federal taxes paid. In assessing the impact of various taxes, individual income taxes are allocated directly to households paying those taxes. Social insurance, or payroll, taxes are allocated to households paying those taxes directly or paying them indirectly through their employers. Corporate income taxes are allocated to households according to their share of capital income. Federal excise taxes are allocated to households according to their consumption of the taxed good or service.

Average tax rates are calculated by dividing federal taxes paid by the sum of market income and transfer income. Negative tax rates result when refundable tax credits, such as the earned income and child tax credits, exceed the other taxes owed by people in an income group. (Refundable tax credits are not limited to the amount of income tax owed before they are applied.)

The *Gini index* is a summary measure of income inequality based on the relationship between shares of income and shares of the population. It ranges in value from zero to one, with zero indicating complete equality (for example, if each fifth of the population, ranked by income, received one-fifth of total income) and one indicating complete inequality (for example, if one household received all the income). A Gini index that increases over time indicates rising income dispersion.

A *concentration index* is a measure similar to a Gini coefficient and is used in this study to express the inequality of market income from different sources. The index differs from a Gini index for an income source because in calculating the concentration index, households are ranked by total market income rather than by income from that source, as they would be in calculating the Gini index for that income source.

PREFACE

This Congressional Budget Office (CBO) study—prepared at the request of the Chairman and former Ranking Member of the Senate Committee on Finance—documents changes in the distribution of household income between 1979 and 2007. CBO's analysis examines the distribution of household income before and after government transfers and federal taxes, and it reports the contribution of various income components (such as wages and salaries, capital income, and business income) to the distribution of market income.

The study presents information on trends in the distribution of income for all households combined and for households separated on the basis of age and the presence of children. In keeping with CBO's mandate to provide objective, impartial analysis, this study makes no recommendations.

Edward Harris and Frank Sammartino of CBO's Tax Analysis Division wrote the study. Greg Acs, Nabeel Alsalam, Mark Hadley, Jon Schwabish, and David Weiner, all of CBO, provided helpful comments, as did Sheldon Danziger of the University of Michigan and Tom DeLeire and Tim Smeeding of the University of Wisconsin-Madison. The assistance of external reviewers implies no responsibility for the final product, which rests solely with CBO.

Christine Bogusz edited the study, and Sherry Snyder proofread it. Jeanine Rees prepared the study for publication, and Maureen Costantino designed the cover. Monte Ruffin printed the initial copies, and Linda Schimmel coordinated the print distribution.

Douglas W. Elmendorf
Director
October 2011

SUMMARY

From 1979 to 2007, real (inflation-adjusted) average household income, measured after government transfers and federal taxes, grew by 62 percent. During that period, the evolution of the nation's economy and the tax and spending policies of the federal government and state and local governments had varying effects on households at different points in the income distribution: Income after transfers and federal taxes (denoted as after-tax income in this study) for households at the higher end of the income scale rose much more rapidly than income for households in the middle and at the lower end of the income scale.[1] In particular:

- For the 1 percent of the population with the highest income, average real after-tax household income grew by 275 percent between 1979 and 2007 (see Summary Figure 1).

- For others in the 20 percent of the population with the highest income (those in the 81st through 99th percentiles), average real after-tax household income grew by 65 percent over that period, much faster than it did for the remaining 80 percent of the population, but not nearly as fast as for the top 1 percent.

- For the 60 percent of the population in the middle of the income scale (the 21st through 80th percentiles), the growth in average real after-tax household income was just under 40 percent.

- For the 20 percent of the population with the lowest income, average real after-tax household income was about 18 percent higher in 2007 than it had been in 1979.

As a result of that uneven income growth, the distribution of after-tax household income in the United States was substantially more unequal in 2007 than in 1979: The share of income accruing to higher-income households increased, whereas the share accruing to other households declined. In fact, between 2005 and 2007, the after-tax income received by the 20 percent of the population with the highest income exceeded the after-tax income of the remaining 80 percent.

To assess trends in the distribution of household income, the Congressional Budget Office (CBO) examined the span from 1979 to 2007 because those endpoints allow comparisons between periods of similar overall economic activity (they were both years before recessions). The growth in average income for different groups over the 1979–2007 period reflects a comparison of average income for those groups at different points in time; it does not reflect the experience of particular households. Individual households may have moved up or down the income scale if their income rose or fell more than the average for their initial group. Thus, the population with income in the lowest 20 percent in 2007 was not necessarily the same as the population in that category in 1979.

Increased Concentration of Market Income

The major reason for the growing unevenness in the distribution of after-tax income was an increase in the concentration of market income (income measured before government transfers and taxes) in favor of higher-income households; that is, such households' share of market income was greater in 2007 than in 1979. Specifically, over that period, the highest income quintile's share of market income increased from 50 percent to 60 percent (see Summary Figure 2). The share of market income for every other quintile declined. (Each quintile contains one-fifth of the population, ranked by adjusted household income.) In fact, the distribution of market income became more unequal almost continuously between 1979 and 2007 except during the recessions in 1990–1991 and 2001.

Two factors accounted for the changing distribution of market income. One was an increase in the concentration of each source of market income, which consists of labor income (such as cash wages and salaries and employer-paid health insurance premiums), business income, capital gains, capital income, and other income. All of those sources of market income were less evenly distributed in 2007 than they were in 1979.

The other factor leading to an increased concentration of market income was a shift in the composition of that income. Labor income has been more evenly distributed than capital and business income, and both capital income and business income have been more evenly distributed than capital gains.

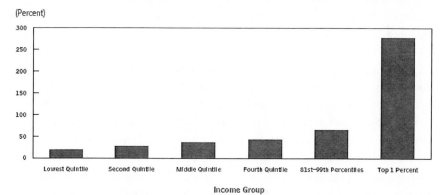

(Percent)

Income Group

Source: Congressional Budget Office.
Note: For information on income definitions, the ranking of households, the allocation of taxes, and the construction of inequality indexes, see "Notes and Definitions" at the beginning of this study.

Summary Figure 1. Growth in Real After-Tax Income from 1979 to 2007.

Between 1979 and 2007, the share of income coming from capital gains and business income increased, while the share coming from labor income and capital income decreased.

Those two factors were responsible in varying degrees for the increase in income concentration over different portions of the 1979–2007 period. In the early years of the period, market income concentration increased almost exclusively as a result of an increasing concentration of separate income sources. The increased concentration of labor income alone accounted for more than 90 percent of the increase in the concentration of market income in those years. In the middle years of the period, an increase in the concentration within each income source accounted for about one-half of the overall increase in market income concentration; a shift to more-concentrated sources explains the other half. In the later years, an increase in the share of total income from more highly concentrated sources, in this case capital gains, accounted for about four-fifths of the total increase in concentration. Over the 1979–2007 period as a whole, an increasing concentration of each source of market income was the more significant factor, accounting for four-fifths of the increase in market income concentration.

Income at the Very Top of the Distribution

The rapid growth in average real household market income for the 1 percent of the population with the highest income was a major factor contributing to the growing inequality in the distribution of household income between 1979 and 2007. Average real household market income for the highest income group nearly tripled over that period, whereas market income increased by about 19 percent for a household at the midpoint of the income distribution. As a result of that uneven growth, the share of total market income received by the top 1 percent of the population more than doubled between 1979 and 2007, growing from about 10 percent to more than 20 percent. Without that growth at the top of the distribution, income inequality still would have increased, but not by nearly as much.

The precise reasons for the rapid growth in income at the top are not well understood, though researchers have offered several potential rationales, including technical innovations that have changed the labor market for superstars (such as actors, athletes, and musicians), changes in the governance and structure of executive compensation, increases in firms' size and complexity, and the increasing scale of financial-sector activities.

The composition of income for the 1 percent of the population with the highest income changed significantly from 1979 to 2007, as the shares from labor and business income increased and the share of income represented by capital income decreased. That pattern is consistent with a longer-term trend: Over the entire 20th century, labor income has become a larger share of income for high-income taxpayers, while capital income has declined as a share of their income.

(Percent)

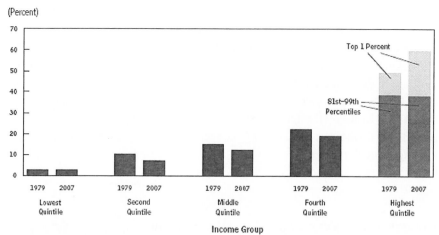

Source: Congressional Budget Office.

Note: For information on income definitions, the ranking of households, the allocation of taxes, and the construction of inequality indexes, see "Notes and Definitions" at the beginning of this study.

Summary Figure 2.. Shares of Market Income, 1979 and 2007.

The precise reasons for the rapid growth in income at the top are not well understood, though researchers have offered several potential rationales, including technical innovations that have changed the labor market for superstars (such as actors, athletes, and musicians), changes in the governance and structure of executive compensation, increases in firms' size and complexity, and the increasing scale of financial-sector activities.

The composition of income for the 1 percent of the population with the highest income changed significantly from 1979 to 2007, as the shares from labor and business income increased and the share of income represented by capital income decreased. That pattern is consistent with a longer-term trend: Over the entire 20th century, labor income has become a larger share of income for high-income taxpayers, while capital income has declined as a share of their income.

The Role of Government Transfers and Federal Taxes

Although an increasing concentration of market income was the primary force behind growing inequality in the distribution of after-tax household income, shifts in government transfers (cash payments to individuals and estimates of the value of in-kind benefits) and federal taxes also contributed to that increase in inequality.[2] CBO estimates that the dispersion of market income grew by about one-quarter between 1979 and 2007, while the dispersion of after-tax income grew by about one-third.[3]

This study assesses the effects of transfers and taxes on the distribution of household income by examining the differences in the dispersion of income for three types of income:

- Market income (before-transfer, before-tax income),
- Market income plus government transfers (after-transfer, before-tax income), and
- Market income plus government transfers minus federal taxes (after-transfer, after-federal-tax income)—called after-tax income in this study.

A proportional transfer and tax system would leave the dispersion of after-tax income equal to the dispersion of market income. Transfers that are a decreasing percentage of market income as income rises (progressive transfers) cause after-tax income to be less concentrated than market income, as do taxes that are an increasing percentage of before-tax household income as income rises (progressive taxes).

Transfers and taxes can also affect households' market income by creating incentives for people to change their behavior. If an additional dollar earned or saved leads to reductions in transfer payments or increases in taxes, then the after-tax return to working and saving is reduced, which may cause people to work or save less. However, those changes in transfers and taxes also reduce after-transfer, after-tax income, which may cause people to work or save more. In this analysis, CBO did not adjust market income to account for those effects of transfers and taxes.

Because government transfers and federal taxes are both progressive, the distribution of after-transfer, afterfederal-tax household income is more equal than is the distribution of market income. Specifically, the dispersion of after-tax income in 2007 was about four-fifths as large as the dispersion of market income. Of the difference in dispersion between market income and after-tax income, roughly 60 percent was attributable to transfers and roughly 40 percent was attributable to federal taxes.

The equalizing effect of transfers and taxes on household income was smaller in 2007 than it had been in 1979. The equalizing effect of transfers depends on their size relative to market income and their distribution across

the income scale. The size of transfer payments—as measured in this study—
rose by a small amount between 1979 and 2007. The distribution of transfers
shifted, however, moving away from households in the lower part of the
income scale. In 1979, households in the bottom quintile received more than
50 percent of transfer payments. In 2007, similar households received about 35
percent of transfers. That shift reflects the growth in spending for programs
focused on the elderly population (such as Social Security and Medicare), in
which benefits are not limited to low-income households. As a result,
government transfers reduced the dispersion of household income by less in
2007 than in 1979.

Likewise, the equalizing effect of federal taxes depends on both the
amount of federal taxes relative to income (the average tax rate) and the
distribution of taxes among households at different income levels. Over the
1979– 2007 period, the overall average federal tax rate fell by a small amount,
the composition of federal revenues shifted away from progressive income
taxes to less-progressive payroll taxes, and income taxes became slightly more
concentrated at the higher end of the income scale. The effect of the first two
factors outweighed the effect of the third, reducing the extent to which taxes
lessened the dispersion of household income.

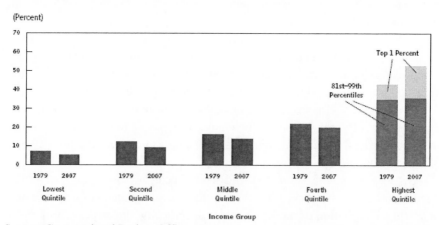

Source: Congressional Budget Office.

Note: For information on income definitions, the ranking of households, the allocation
   of taxes, and the construction of inequality indexes, see "Notes and Definitions" at
   the beginning of this study.

Summary Figure 3. Shares of Income After Transfers and Federal Taxes, 1979 and
2007.

Increased Concentration of after-Tax Income

As a result of those changes, the share of household income after transfers and federal taxes going to the highest income quintile grew from 43 percent in 1979 to 53 percent in 2007 (see Summary Figure 3). The share of after-tax household income for the 1 percent of the population with the highest income more than doubled, climbing from nearly 8 percent in 1979 to 17 percent in 2007.

The population in the lowest income quintile received about 7 percent of after-tax income in 1979; by 2007, their share of after-tax income had fallen to about 5 percent. The middle three income quintiles all saw their shares of after-tax income decline by 2 to 3 percentage points between 1979 and 2007.

TRENDS IN THE DISTRIBUTION OF HOUSEHOLD INCOME BETWEEN 1979 AND 2007

Introduction

This Congressional Budget Office (CBO) analysis finds that, over the past three decades, the distribution of income in the United States has become increasingly dispersed—in particular, the share of income accruing to higher-income households has increased, whereas the share accruing to other households has declined. Despite definitional and methodological differences, other analyses using data from tax returns or surveys have reached similar conclusions.[1]

The dispersion of household income rose almost continually throughout the nearly 30-year period spanning 1979 through 2007 except during the 1990–1991 and 2001 recessions. The recent turmoil in financial markets, the prolonged recession that began in December 2007, and the ongoing slow recovery may have caused a pause in that upward trend, but the present analysis does not extend beyond 2007.[2]

Other developed economies have experienced a similar long-term trend toward greater dispersion in household income. A recent report covering the 30 developed countries of the Organization for Economic Cooperation and Development (OECD) concluded, "Overall, over the entire period from the mid-1980s to the mid-2000s, the dominant pattern is one of a fairly widespread increase in inequality (in two-thirds of all countries) . . . The rises are stronger in Finland, Norway and Sweden (from a low base) as well as Germany, Italy, New Zealand and the United States (from a higher base)."[3]

The growing dispersion of household income over the past three decades follows a lengthy period in which income concentration was little changed. Economists Thomas Piketty and Emmanuel Saez used data from tax returns to examine income concentration in the United States over the past 90 years. They found that income concentration dropped dramatically following World War I and World War II, remained roughly unchanged for the next few decades, and then rose starting in 1975, reaching pre–World War I levels by 2000.[4]

CBO's Analysis

In this analysis, CBO examines the trends in the distribution of household income from 1979 through 2007. Using data from the Internal Revenue Service (IRS) and survey data collected by the Census Bureau, CBO estimated income after government transfer payments and federal taxes for a representative sample of households in each year during that period. (Appendix A contains a more detailed discussion of the data and methodology.) CBO analyzed the trend in the dispersion of households' after-transfer, after-federal-tax income (in this study, labeled "after-tax income") and the extent to which transfers and federal taxes mitigated the dispersion of before-transfer, before-tax income (in this report, labeled "market income"). The analysis examines the contribution of various components of income—such as wages and salaries, capital income, and business income—to the distribution of market income and considers the effects of increases in women's participation in the labor force and women's earnings. It presents information on the trends in the distribution of income for all households combined and for households separated on the basis of age and the presence of children.

The beginning and end points of the analysis, 1979 and 2007, were similar years in terms of overall economic activity; both were economic peak years just prior to a recession.[5] Moreover, as a practical matter, 1979 is the earliest year for which the Census Bureau provides consistent estimates for some measures of income.

CBO focuses on annual income measures in this analysis, comparing average income at different points in time for different households grouped by income or household type. However, many households represented in those averages experienced growth or declines in income that differed from the average experience for their initial group, and the households in any particular segment of the income distribution in 2007 were not necessarily the same households that were in that segment in 1979.

(Percentage change in income since 1979, adjusted for inflation)

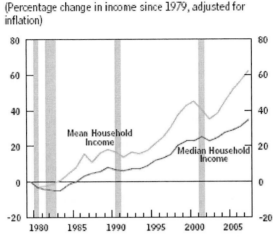

Source: Congressional Budget Office.
Note: For information on income definitions, the ranking of households, the allocation of taxes, and the construction of inequality indexes, see "Notes and Definitions" at the beginning of this study.

Figure 1. Cumulative Growth in Mean and Median Household After-Tax Income.

The analysis does not assess trends in the distribution of other measures of economic well-being, such as household income measured over a longer period, household consumption, or household wealth (see Box 1).

Increased Dispersion of Households' after-Tax Income

Real (inflation-adjusted) *mean* household income, measured after government transfers and federal taxes, grew by 62 percent between 1979 and 2007. Over the same period, real *median* after-tax household income (half of all households have income below the median, and half have income above it) grew by 35 percent (see Figure 1). Because the mean (or average) can be heavily influenced by very high or very low incomes, the large gap between

mean and median income growth signals a pattern of growth that was heavily
weighted toward households with income well above the median.

Uneven Growth in after-Tax Income

The distribution of after-tax income (including government transfer
payments) became substantially more unequal from 1979 to 2007 as a result of a
rapid rise in income for the highest-income households, sluggish income growth
for the middle 60 percent of the population, and an even smaller increase in after-tax
income for the 20 percent of the population with the lowest income.[6]

Average real after-tax household income for the 1 percent of the
population with the highest income grew by 275 percent between 1979 and
2007 (see Figure 2). Average real after-tax income for that group has been
quite volatile:

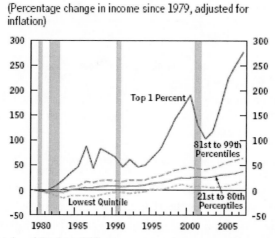

(Percentage change in income since 1979, adjusted for
inflation)

Source: Congressional Budget Office.

Note: For information on income definitions, the ranking of households, the allocation
of taxes, and the construction of inequality indexes, see "Notes and Definitions" at
the beginning of this study.

Figure 2. Cumulative Growth in Average After-Tax Income, by Income Group.

It spiked in 1986 and fell in 1987, reflecting an acceleration of capital
gains realizations into 1986 in anticipation of the scheduled increase in tax
rates the following year. Income growth for the top 1 percent of the population
rebounded in 1988 but fell again with the onset of the 1990–1991 recession.
By 1994, after-tax household income was 50 percent higher than it had been in
1979. Income growth surged in 1995, averaging more than 11 percent per year

through 2000. After falling sharply in 2001 because of the recession and stock market drop, average real after-tax income for the top 1 percent of the population rose by more than 85 percent between 2002 and 2007. (The turmoil in financial markets in 2008 probably reversed some of that growth, but it is not clear by how much or for how long.)

For other households in the highest-income quintile (the 81st through 99th percentiles), average after-tax income grew by 65 percent between 1979 and 2007. That growth was not nearly as great as for the top 1 percent of the population, although it was much greater than for most other households.

For the 60 percent of the population in the middle of the income scale (the 21st through 80th percentiles), average after-tax household income grew 37 percent between 1979 and 2007. Income for those households grew in most years starting after 1983, with the exception of 1990–1991 and 2002.

Average after-tax household income in the lowest income quintile (the 1st through 20th percentiles) was 18 percent higher in 2007 than in 1979. After-tax income for that quintile dropped sharply during the 1980 and 1981– 1982 recessions; by 1983, that income was 15 percent lower than it had been in 1979, and it did not rebound to its 1979 level until 1995, some 16 years later. Average after-tax income for the lowest income quintile peaked in 1999, fell through 2003, and then began to rise again in 2004, climbing steadily through 2007.

The Resulting Shift in Income Shares

As a result of that uneven income growth, the share of total after-tax income received by the 1 percent of the population in households with the highest income more than doubled between 1979 and 2007, whereas the share received by low- and middle-income households declined (see Figure 3). The share of income received by the top 1 percent grew from about 8 percent in 1979 to over 17 percent in 2007. The share received by other households in the highest income quintile was fairly flat over the same period, edging up from 35 percent to 36 percent. In contrast, the share of after-tax income received by the 60 percent of the population in the three middle-income quintiles fell by 7 percentage points between 1979 and 2007, from 50 percent to 43 percent of total after-tax household income, and the share of after-tax income accruing to the lowest-income quintile decreased from 7 percent to 5 percent. By 2005, the share of total after-tax household income received by the 20 percent of the population with the highest income had exceeded the share received by the remaining 80 percent. In 2007, those shares were 53 percent and 47 percent, respectively. In 1979, the top 1 percent received about the same share of income as the lowest income quintile; by 2007, the top percentile received more than the lowest two income quintiles combined.

Increased Dispersion of Households' Market Income

An increase in the dispersion of household market income was the major reason for the widening dispersion of household after-tax income.

Box 1. Measures of Economic Well-Being

Because annual income is only one measure of economic well-being, trends in the distribution of annual income may provide an incomplete picture of trends in the distribution of well-being. For example, a household's income in any given year may not accurately represent its economic circumstances over a longer period. Average income over multiple years, even over a lifetime, might be a better indicator of a household's economic well-being.

Likewise, a household's consumption might be a better measure of its economic well-being than its income is. For households whose spending tracks their annual income, the distinction does not matter. But a young family may spend more than its current income, relying on borrowing to finance current consumption, while an older family may also spend more than its current income, drawing down assets in retirement. In contrast, a household in its middle years may spend less than its current income while saving for future needs.

The ability of households to smooth their consumption over time by borrowing and saving suggests that household wealth might provide another useful perspective on economic well-being. Households may finance consumption directly from accumulated wealth by drawing down assets or by borrowing with those assets as collateral. In addition, some forms of wealth, such as owner-occupied housing, provide a service to owners that is often not measured as part of annual income.

Those alternative measures of economic well-being— household income measured over a longer time, household consumption, and household wealth—are distributed across households in different ways than annual income is. Moreover, the distributions of those measures may have evolved in different ways than has the distribution of households' annual income over the past three decades.

Household income measured over a multiyear period is more equally distributed than income measured over one year, although only modestly so. Given the fairly substantial movement of households across income groups over time, it might seem that income measured over a number of years should be significantly more equally distributed than income measured over one year. However, much of the movement of households involves changes in income that are large enough to push households into different income groups but not large enough to greatly affect the overall distribution of income.

Multiyear income measures also show the same pattern of increasing inequality over time as is observed in annual measures.[1]

Household consumption is more equally distributed than household income. Trends in the concentration of household consumption are mixed. Inequality in consumption appears to have increased during the 1980s but not in the 1990s.[2] However, data on the consumption of U.S. households do not adequately capture consumption by high-income households, a group whose rising income accounts for much of the observed increase in annual income inequality.

Household wealth is much more unequally distributed than household income or household consumption. The distribution of household wealth appears to have become more unequal from 1983 to 1989 but to have remained relatively unchanged from 1989 through 2007.[3]

---

[1]. Congressional Budget Office, *Effective Tax Rates: Comparing Annual and Multiyear Measures* (January 2005); and Wojciech Kopczuk, Emmanuel Saez, and Jae Song, "Earnings Inequality and Mobility in the United States: Evidence from Social Security Data Since 1937," *Quarterly Journal of Economics,* vol. 125, no. 1 (February 2010), pp. 91–128.

[2]. For further discussion, see David M. Cutler and Lawrence F. Katz, "Rising Inequality? Changes in the Distribution of Income and Consumption in the 1980s," *American Economic Review*, vol. 82, no. 2 (1992), pp. 546–551; David S. Johnson, Timothy M. Smeeding, and Barbara Boyle Torrey, "Economic Inequality Through the Prisms of Income and Consumption," *Monthly Labor Review*, vol. 128, no. 4 (2005), pp. 11–24; and Dirk Krueger and Fabrizio Perri, "Does Income Inequality Lead to Consumption Inequality? Evidence and Theory," *Review of Economic Studies*, vol. 73, no. 1 (2006), pp. 163–193.

[3]. For further discussion, see Wojciech Kopczuk and Emmanuel Saez, "Top Wealth Shares in the United States, 1916– 2000: Evidence from Estate Tax Returns," *National Tax Journal*, vol. 57, no. 2, part 2 (2004), pp. 445–488.

Market income is measured before adding transfer payments and subtracting federal taxes and consists of labor income (such as cash wages and salaries and employer-paid health insurance premiums), business income, capital gains, capital income, and other income. Real average market income grew by 58 percent between 1979 and 2007 (similar to the 62 percent change in average after-tax income), but median market income grew by only 19 percent (less than the 35 percent growth in median after-tax income; see Figure 4).

Measuring Income Dispersion

Various summary measures of income dispersion condense data for the entire distribution of household income into a single number. One such measure, the Gini index, is based on the relationship between shares of income and shares of the population (see Box 2). That index ranges in value from zero to one, with zero indicating complete equality (for example, if each percentile of the population, ranked by income, received 1 percent of total income) and one indicating complete inequality (for example, if one household received all the income). A Gini index for household income that increases over time indicates rising inequality of household income.

The Gini index for household market income rose from 0.479 in 1979 to 0.590 by 2007, an increase of 23 percent (see Figure 5).[7] The index increased almost continuously during that span except for declines during the recessions in 1990–1991 and 2001. The rate of increase was not constant, however. The Gini index increased at a rate of about 11/4 percent per year from 1979 through 1988, at about 1 percent per year from 1991 through 2000, and at a 2 percent annual rate from 2002 through 2005; it changed little from 2005 through 2007.

The Gini index also can be described another way, as half of the average difference in income between every pair of households in the population, expressed as a percentage of average income. From that perspective, a Gini index of 0.479 in 1979 implies that the average income difference between pairs of households in that year was equal to 96 percent (twice 0.479) of average household market income, or about $34,500 (measured in constant 2007 dollars and adjusted for differences in household size). Similarly, a Gini index of 0.590 in 2007 implies that the average difference between pairs of households was 118 percent (twice 0.590) of average household market income in that year, or about $66,600 (with a similar adjustment for household size).

Some of the transitory changes in the Gini index reflect the volatile nature of income from capital gains. Capital gains ranged from about 3 percent to 5 percent of market income in most years, but they spiked to over 10 percent in 1986 and nearly 9 percent in 2000. The spike in 1986 reflected the rush to realize profits from increases in asset prices in anticipation of the tax-rate increase scheduled to take effect in 1987. The peak in 2000 was the cul-mination of five years of growing realizations reflecting the run-up in stock market prices from 1995 through 2000. Realized gains peaked again in 2007, at 9 percent of market income.

Removing capital gains from before-transfer, before-tax income smoothes out some of the jumps in the Gini measure but does not change the trend (see Figure 5).

The Gini index for market income excluding capital gains increased from 0.464 to 0.562 between 1979 and 2007.

That increase of more than 21 percent was nearly as large as the 23 per-cent increase in the Gini index for household income including capital gains.

Comparison with Other Estimates

Other researchers have reached similar conclusions about the trends in income inequality. In an influential paper, economists Thomas Piketty and Emmanuel Saez found that income concentration began to rise in the late 1970s and continued to grow thereafter. They found especially dramatic increases within the top percentile of the income distribution[8]. Their analysis is based on published tax return statistics, and it uses a market-income definition.

The key advantage of those data, as well as the data used in this analysis, is that they are comprehensive at the top of the income distribution, where much of the change in the income distribution has occurred. One drawback of tax return data alone, however, is that they only cover the portion of the population filing tax returns, so they cannot yield distributional statistics for the full population. In addition, they cannot capture income that is not reported on tax returns.

Census Bureau statistics also show an increase in inequality, although those statistics—which do not measure income for the highest-income households nearly as well as tax return data—imply both a smaller degree of inequality and a smaller increase in inequality than were found in CBO's analysis. As computed by the Census Bureau, the Gini index for household money income—a before-tax income measure that includes some government transfers—rose from 0.403 in 1979 to 0.463 in 2007, an increase of 15 percent.[9] The Gini indexes for alternative measures of income (as computed by the Census Bureau) show comparable increases.

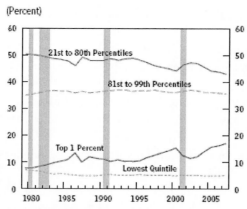

Source: Congressional Budget Office.
Note: For information on income definitions, the ranking of households, the allocation of taxes, and the construction of inequality indexes, see "Notes and Definitions" at the beginning of this study.

Figure 3. Share of Total After-Tax Income, by Income Group.

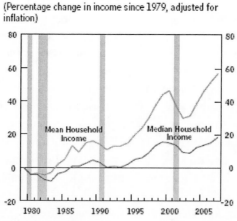

Source: Congressional Budget Office.
Note: For information on income definitions, the ranking of households, the allocation of taxes, and the construction of inequality indexes, see "Notes and Definitions" at the beginning of this study.

Figure 4. Cumulative Growth in Mean and Median Household Market Income

(Gini index)

Source: Congressional Budget Office.

Note: For information on income definitions, the ranking of households, the allocation of taxes, and the construction of inequality indexes, see "Notes and Definitions" at the beginning of this study.

Figure 5. Summary Measures of Market Income Inequality, With and Without Capital Gains.

Economist Richard Burkhauser and his coauthors, using internal Census Bureau data, found that the rate of increase in inequality has slowed substantially since the mid-1990s.[10] They computed Gini indexes using a before-tax, after-transfer measure of household cash income, excluding capital gains, which was adjusted for differences in household size using the square root of household size. They found that the Gini index grew at an annual rate of 0.14 percent after 1993, in contrast to a growth rate of 0.74 percent in the 1975–1992 period.

Burkhauser and his coauthors also compared the trends in top income shares with those reported by Piketty and Saez and found that the measures from the two data sources align well, except for measures for the top percentile of the income distribution. Even though Burkhauser and his coauthors found little increase in income inequality after 1993, their analysis did not reject the possibility that inequality could have increased among the highestincome households, so they concluded that their results were not inconsistent with those of Piketty and Saez.

An increase among the highest-income households may explain the slower growth in measured income inequality in more recent years in the Census Bureau's data.

Why Did Market Income Become Less Equally Distributed?

The market income of households can become more unequally distributed over time if individual components of income become more highly concentrated or if the composition of income shifts so that a greater share of total income comes from components that are more highly concentrated.

Over the 1979–2007 period, the first of those factors was the primary reason overall market income became less evenly distributed: All major sources of market income became more highly concentrated in favor of higher-income households. Labor income was the biggest contributor because it is by far the largest source of income, even though the increase in the concentration of labor income was smaller than the increase in concentration for other sources.

A shift in the composition of income also contributed to the growing concentration.

Box 2. Calculating and Interpreting the Gini Index
Income and Population Shares, 2007

(Percent) Income Group		Population		Market Income		After-Tax Income (Income After Transfers and Federal Taxes)	
	Share	Cumulative Share	Share	Cumulative Share	Share	Cumulative Share
Lowest Quintile	20	20	2	2	4	4
Second Quintile	20	40	7	9	9	13
Middle Quintile	20	60	12	21	14	27
Fourth Quintile	20	80	19	40	20	47
81st–90th Percentiles	10	90	14	55	14	61
91st–95th Percentiles	5	95	10	65	10	71
96th–99th Percentiles	4	99	14	79	12	83
Top 1 Percent	1	100	21	100	17	100

Source: Congressional Budget Office.

Note: For information on income definitions, the ranking of households, the allocation of taxes, and the construction of inequality indexes, see "Notes and Definitions" at the beginning of this study.

The Gini index is a widely used measure of income inequality. It ranges from zero to one, with higher values implying greater inequality. The index provides a useful summary metric of the entire income distribution by characterizing it with a single number, but interpreting the value of the index may not be intuitive.

The Gini index can be estimated directly from data on the shares of income accruing to various groups.[1] The first step in computing the index is to array the groups in order from lowest to highest income and to calculate the share of income earned by each group. Consider the distribution of market income (defined here as income before transfers and taxes) in 2007. The lowest quintile (or one-fifth of the population) earned 2 percent of market income; the second middle, and fourth quintiles earned 7 percent, 12 percent, and 19 percent, respectively; and the remaining 60 percent of market income was divided among the subgroups of the top quintile (see the table).

The distribution of income after transfers and federal taxes (labeled after-tax income) was more equal than was the distribution of market income. Each of the bottom four quintiles (ranked by after-tax income) received a share of after-tax income that was 1 or 2 percentage points higher than its share of market income, while the highest quintile's share of after-tax income was 6 percentage points lower than its share of market income.

The next step in calculating the index is to compute the cumulative share of income earned by each group and all of the groups with lower income. The first and second quintiles—cumulatively, the bottom 40 percent of the population—received a combined 9 percent of market income and 13 percent of after-tax income. Adding the middle quintile shows that the bottom 60 percent of the population received 21 percent of market income and 27 percent of after-tax income.

The cumulative percentage of income can be plotted against the cumulative percentage of the population, producing a so-called Lorenz curve (see the figure).

The more even the income distribution is, the closer to a 45-degree line the Lorenz curve is. At one extreme, if each income group had the same income, then the cumulative income share would equal the cumulative population share, and the Lorenz curve would follow the 45-degree line, known as the line of equality.

At the other extreme, if the highest income group earned all the income, the Lorenz curve would be flat across the vast majority of the income range, following the bottom edge of the figure, and then jump to the top of the figure at the very right-hand edge.

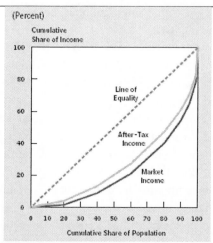

Source: Congressional Budget Office.

Notes: For information on income definitions, the ranking of households, the allocation of taxes, and the construction of inequality indexes, see "Notes and Definitions" at the beginning of this study. The line of equality shows what the distribution would be if each income group had equal income.

Lorenz curves for actual income distributions fall between those two hypothetical extremes. Typically, they intersect the diagonal line only at the very first and last points. Between those points, the curves are bow-shaped below the 45-degree line. The Lorenz curve of market income falls to the right and below the curve for after-tax income, reflecting its greater inequality. Both curves fall to the right and below the line of equality, reflecting the inequality in both market income and after-tax income.

The Gini index is equal to twice the area between the 45-degree line and the Lorenz curve. Once again, the extreme cases of complete equality and complete inequality bound the measure.

At one extreme, if income was evenly distributed and the Lorenz curve followed the 45-degree line, there would be no area between the curve and the line, so the Gini index would be zero. At the other extreme, if all income was in the highest income group, the area between the line and the curve would be equal to the entire area under the line, and the Gini index would equal one. The Gini index for after-tax income in 2007 was 0.489—about halfway between those two extremes.

1. To calculate the Gini indexes in the primary analysis, the Congressional Budget Office applied this approach to disaggregated data, yielding a more precise estimate of the Gini index than do calculations based on grouped data.

A decrease in the share of total market income from wages and other labor compensation and an increase in the share from capital gains contributed to the increase in market income inequality because capital gains are much more concentrated among higher-income households than is labor income.

Sources of Income

For this analysis, CBO divided market income into the following components:

- *Labor income:* Cash wages and salaries (including those allocated by employees to 401(k) plans), employer-paid health insurance premiums, and the employer's share of Social Security, Medicare, and federal unemployment insurance payroll taxes. CBO assumes in this analysis that the employer's share of payroll taxes is passed on to employees in the form of lower wages and, therefore, that those taxes are effectively being paid by the employees and should be included in before-transfer, before-tax household income.

- *Business income:* Net income from businesses and farms operated solely by their owners, partnership income, and income from S corporations. (Corporations can elect S corporation status if they have 100 or fewer shareholders and meet certain other requirements. S corporations do not pay the corporate income tax but instead must pass through all income and losses to shareholders.)

- *Capital gains:* Profits realized from the sale of assets. Increases in the value of assets that have not been realized through sales are not included in market income.

- *Capital income* (excluding capital gains): Taxable and tax-exempt interest, dividends paid by corporations (but not dividends from S corporations, which are considered part of business income), rental income, and corporate income taxes. CBO assumes in this analysis that corporate income taxes are borne by owners of capital in proportion to their income from capital; therefore, the imputed amount of the corporate tax is included in household income measured before taxes.

- *Other income:* Income received in retirement for past services and any other sources of income.

Labor income accounted for more than 70 percent of market income in most years between 1979 and 2007, although its share of total income had dropped from three-fourths in 1979 to two-thirds by 2007. Capital income (excluding capital gains) is the next largest source, but even at its peak in 1981 it was only about 14 percent of market income. After that, the share of total income from capital declined to about 10 percent of total income in 2007. Income from capital gains rose from about 4 percent of market income in 1979 to about 8 percent in 2007. Business income and income from other sources (primarily private pensions) each accounted for about 7 percent of total income in 2007, up from about 4 percent apiece in 1979.

The Distribution of Various Income Sources

Labor income is more evenly distributed across the income spectrum than business income and capital income, both of which are more evenly distributed than capital gains. In 1979, the bottom 80 percent of the population in the income spectrum received nearly 60 percent of total labor income, about 33 percent of income from capital and business, and about 8 percent from capital gains (see Figure 6). By 2007, the share of labor income going to the bottom 80 percent had dropped to less than 50 percent, their percentage of business income and income from capital had decreased to 20 percent, and their share of capital gains was about 5 percent. All sources of income were less evenly distributed in 2007 than in 1979.

A concentration index can express the concentration of each income source as a single number. It is analogous to a Gini index, and rising values signify rising concentration of income.[11]

Concentration indexes for the major sources of income all increased—albeit irregularly—from 1979 to 2007, indicating rising dispersion in the distribution of each source of income (see Figure 7). Labor income became steadily more concentrated from 1979 through 1988, and then again in 1992 following the 1990–1991 recession. After remaining mostly unchanged during the rest of the 1990s, the concentration of labor income increased again from 1999 through 2002. Since 2002, the concentration has declined slightly, though not back to the levels of the late 1990s.

Capital income became increasingly concentrated beginning in the early 1990s. After declines in 2001 and 2002, its concentration then increased significantly from 2003 through 2007. Capital gains also became increasingly concentrated beginning in the early 1990s; unlike other income from capital, however, the degree of concentration of capital gains continued to rise through 2003 but fell thereafter. The concentration of business income was quite variable in the early part of the 1980s. Some of that variability might reflect changes in tax law in that period. After 1986, the concentration of business income rose steadily through 1991 and then declined through much of the 1990s before rising rapidly in the 2000–2002 period. Since then, the concentration has declined, though not back to the levels that prevailed in the 1990s.

Decomposing Changes in Market Income Inequality by Income Source

A useful property of the Gini index is that it is possible to determine the contribution of different factors to the increase in overall income inequality through a simple decomposition (see Appendix B). The contribution of each income source to the Gini index for total market income is the product of the concentration index for that income source and the share of total market income attributable to that source. Thus, changes in the concentration of income from a source such as labor income will have a much greater effect on overall income concentration than an equivalent change in the concentration of another income source (such as capital income) because labor income is a much larger share of total income.

In contrast, from 1991 to 2000—a period that saw an increase of 4.8 percentage points in the Gini index—a shift to more concentrated sources explains about 45 percent of the overall increase in market income inequality, and an increase in the concentration within each source accounts for the other 55 percent. In that case, a decrease in the percentage of total income from labor and capital and an increase in the share from capital gains were major factors, as were increases in the concentration of both labor and capital income.

The importance of those various factors to the increase of 3.6 percentage points in the Gini index for total market income between 2002 and 2007 differs yet again. More than four-fifths of the total increase in the Gini index over those years stemmed from an increase in the share of total income coming from more highly concentrated capital gains. An increase in the concentration of capital income accounts for most of the remaining increase. Labor income became somewhat less concentrated over that period, but the effect on overall income dispersion was small.

Over the 1979–2007 period as a whole, the increased concentration of the individual sources of market income accounted for close to 80 percent of the total increase in the Gini index.

Why Has the Distribution of Labor Income Grown More Unequal?

Many studies have documented the increasing inequality of labor income, and the result is robust across data sources and statistical measures. In all likelihood, the interaction of multiple factors has led to the growth in labor income inequality, and disentangling the contribution of those factors will remain a focus of research for some time. Most studies have concentrated on the distribution of cash labor income (CBO uses a broader measure of labor income that also includes some forms of nonwage compensation). Cash labor income is determined by multiple factors—hourly wages (the amount earned by workers per hour worked), the number of hours worked per person in the labor force, and the labor market participation of different members of a household. Of those factors, increases in the inequality of hourly wage rates appear to be the largest contributor to the increased inequality of cash labor income. That trend in the distribution of hourly wages stems primarily from a growing demand for skilled workers relative to the supply of such workers.

Hourly Wage Rates

Hourly wages grew more unequal over the 1979–2009 period, but the pattern of growth varied considerably over time, according to a recent CBO study.[12] For men and women alike, the gap between the wage rates received by high-wage workers (those at the 90th percentile of the wage distribution) and middle-wage workers (those at the 50th percentile) grew throughout the 30-year period. The gap between the wage rates received by low-wage workers (those at the 10th percentile of the wage distribution) and middle-wage workers widened somewhat during the 1980s, but not since then.

Numerous researchers have concluded that, on balance, the technological changes of the past several decades— and perhaps the entire past century— increased employers' demand for workers with higher skills and more education. That increase, along with a smaller increase in the supply of workers with higher skills and more education, generated substantial gains in the relative wages of more-educated workers.

Specifically, researchers have argued that the *demand* for skilled workers, particularly for highly educated workers, was spurred by innovations in information and computing technology in the 1990s and 2000s. Moreover, innovations in the production process—such as new technology and organizational changes—also may have increased the productivity of higher-skilled workers more than that of lower-skilled workers.

(Cumulative share of income, in percent)

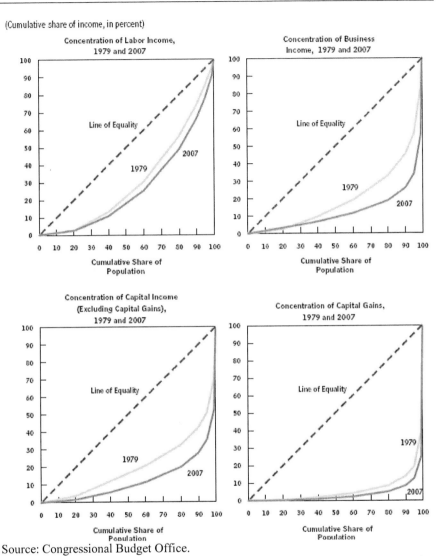

Source: Congressional Budget Office.

Notes: For information on income definitions, the ranking of households, the allocation of taxes, and the construction of inequality indexes, see "Notes and Definitions" at the beginning of this study. The line of equality shows what the distribution would be if each income group had equal income. The concentration curves exclude business and investment losses.

Figure 6. Concentration of Major Sources of Market Income, 1979 and 2007.

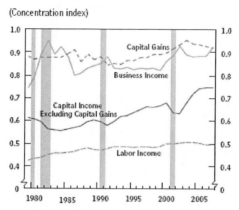

(Concentration index)

Source: Congressional Budget Office.
Note: For information on income definitions, the ranking of households, the allocation of taxes, and the construction of inequality indexes, see "Notes and Definitions" at the beginning of this study.

Figure 7. Income Concentration, by Major Income Source.

Table 1. Sources of Change in the Gini Index for Market Income

	1979 to 1988	1988 to 1991	1991 to 2000	2000 to 2002	2002 to 2007	Total, 1979 to 2007
Change in Gini Index (Percentage points)	5.7	-1.2	4.8	-1.8	3.6	11.1
Source of Change (Percentage points)						
Shift to more or less concentrated income sources	0.4	-0.8	2.2	-2.3	3.1	2.3
Change in concentration within each income source	5.3	-0.3	2.6	0.4	0.5	8.8
Share of Change from Each Source (Percent)						
Shift to more or less concentrated income sources	8	70	45	124	85	21
Change in concentration within each income source	92	30	55	-24	15	79

Source: Congressional Budget Office.
Note: For information on income distributions, the ranking of households, the allocation of taxes, and the construction of inequality indexes, see "Notes and Definitions" at the beginning of this study.

For example, some researchers have hypothesized that information technology might comple-ment highly educated workers engaged in abstract tasks while substituting for moderately educated workers performing routine clerical, mechanical, and analytical tasks. Those researchers have also surmised that the demand for workers performing "low-skilled" service jobs has not been affected because many of those jobs—such as health aides, security guards, orderlies, cleaners, and servers—are not amenable to automation.[13] Owing to those various changes, firms have increased their demand for highly skilled workers.

At the same time, changes in the relative *supplies* of higher- and lower-skilled workers have been more gradual. The growth in the educational attainment of the workforce has slowed, leading to slower growth in the number of higher-skilled workers compared with the number of lower-skilled workers. That change, coupled with the increasing demand for such workers, has led to the rising relative compensation observed in recent decades for skilled and educated people. [14]

Changes in labor market institutions have also contributed to that trend. Some researchers have noted that the early part of the 1979–2006 period saw a substantial decline in the inflation-adjusted value of the minimum wage, which, they argue, accounted for the slower growth in wages at the bottom of the distribution.[15] Other researchers have noted large declines in the rate of unionization in the United States, especially in the 1980s, and have shown that the decline has reduced the equalizing effect of unions on wages.[16]

Developments in trade and immigration may also have affected the distribution of wage rates. The United States has seen increases in both international trade and immigration in recent decades, and the nation has substantially increased its consumption of imported goods. To the extent that imported goods compete with domestic goods produced by lower-skilled workers, an increase in imports would be expected to hold down wages of domestic workers. The empirical research on that effect is inconclusive, however.[17] In addition, changes in the supply of workers attributable to a rising number of foreign-born people in the workforce increase the availability of workers with a broad range of skills, potentially putting downward pressure on wage rates in jobs where they work. Empirical research, however, indicates that the impact of foreign-born workers on wage dispersion has been modest.[18]

Annual Earnings

Another recent CBO study examined the distribution of annual earnings, which is the product of hours worked and wages per hour.[19] That study found that annual earnings have grown more unequal over time for men but not for women and that changes in the number of hours worked have tended to reduce inequality. For men, the ratio of the annual earnings of high earners to those of median earners was larger in 2007 than in 1979, whereas the annual earnings ratio for median and low earners was roughly the same in the two years. Men with the lowest annual earnings increased their work hours somewhat over the period; otherwise, inequality in annual earnings would have grown even more. For women, in contrast, the ratio of the annual earnings of high earners to those of median earners was roughly the same in 2007 as it was in 1979, but the ratio of annual earnings of median earners to those of low earners was smaller in 2007 than it was in 1979. Women at the 10th percentile of their earnings distribution experienced a rapid rise in annual earnings in large part because of increases in the number of hours they worked.

Increases in Women's Labor Force Participation and Earnings

The role of women in the labor market changed dramatically over the time period studied here. Women's participation in the labor force rose rapidly, and the gaps between hourly wage rates and annual earnings for men and women narrowed. In addition, inequality in wage rates among working women grew, though that change was more than offset by changes in hours worked, so inequality of annual earnings did not grow.

Even if the distribution of women's earnings had been unchanged, trends in women's earnings could have changed the inequality of household income. Because married couples tend to have higher income than single people, even after adjusting for differences in household size, an increase in the earnings of women could boost inequality by raising the income of couples relative to that of households headed by single people. The effect of women's earnings on the inequality of household income also depends on the correlation between husbands' and wives' earnings: Relatively faster growth of earnings for women married to men with high earnings would tend to exacerbate the inequality of household income, whereas faster growth of earnings for women married to men with low earnings would tend to decrease it, even holding constant the inequality of women's earnings. Empirical studies on the effect of women's earnings on the inequality of family income have found mixed results, with estimates depending on the period studied and the methodology used.[20]

The data used by CBO in this study are not sufficient for isolating the effect of women's earnings, for two reasons: Sex is not reported in the tax return data, and only the combined earnings of married couples are directly reported on tax returns.[21]

How Did the Distribution of Market Income Change for Different Types of Households?

Trends in market income for the entire population mask significant variations in the amount, composition, and distribution of market income among subgroups of the population. Income dispersion is smaller among households with children (households with at least one member under age 18) and nonelderly childless households (households headed by someone under age 65 with no member under age 18) than among elderly childless households (those headed by someone age 65 or older with no member under age 18) (see Figure 8).

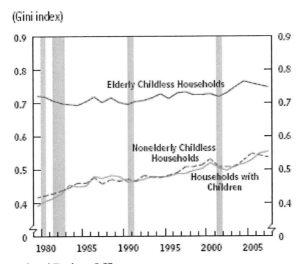

Source: Congressional Budget Office.

Note: For information on income definitions, the ranking of households, the allocation of taxes, and the construction of inequality indexes, see "Notes and Definitions" at the beginning of this study.

Figure 8. Summary Measures of Market Income Inequality for Different Types of Households.

The levels and trends in the dispersion of market income for households with children and nonelderly childless households are virtually identical. Because they account for the majority of households, and an even larger share of market income, the overall trend in market income dispersion closely mirrors that of those two subgroups.

(Gini index)

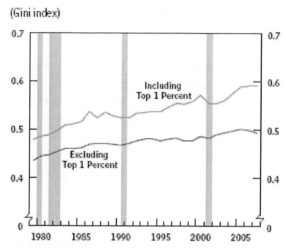

Source: Congressional Budget Office.
Note: For information on income definitions, the ranking of households, the allocation
    of taxes, and the construction of inequality indexes, see "Notes and Definitions" at
    the beginning of this study.

Figure 9. Summary Measures of Market Income Inequality, With and Without the Top
1 Percent of Households.

In contrast, because many elderly people no longer work, the composition
of market income and the extent of market income dispersion among elderly
childless households differ from that of other households. On average,
compared with households headed by the nonelderly, elderly households have
much less labor income and substantially more income from accumulated
savings—in the form of pension income, interest and dividends, and capital
gains. On average, elderly households have less market income than other
households. Indeed, the bottom fifth of elderly childless households has
essentially no market income, and the second fifth has very little. Most of the
income for those groups comes fr om Social Security benefits or other
government transfer programs (which are examined later). And among the
upper three-fifths of the distribution, income is a little more skewed to the top
for elderly childless households than for other types of households. The trend
in income dispersion for elderly childless households has differed from trends
for the rest of the population during the past 30 years. The difference in the
early 1980s is especially striking, when dispersion for elderly childless
households fell while dispersion for other households rose. That period saw an
increase in the concentration of labor income accompanied by a decrease in

the dispersion of capital income. Because many elderly people no longer work, the latter effect was relatively more important for elderly childless households than for the overall population and caused a decline in income inequality among them. The elderly also saw less of an increase in income inequality in the late 1990s, when the dispersion in labor income again grew rapidly.

Changes in Market Income for the Top 1 Percent of the Population

Without the income growth at the very top of the distribution, income dispersion still would have increased, but not by as much (see Figure 9). The Gini index for market income rose from 0.479 in 1979 to 0.590 in 2007, a 23 percent increase. Recalculating the Gini index by excluding the 1 percent of the population in households with the highest income in each year reduces the increase to 14 percent (from about 0.435 in 1979 to 0.495 in 2007).[22]

Composition of Income for the Top 1 Percent of the Population

Between 1979 and 2007, the composition of market income for the 1 percent of the population in households with the highest income changed significantly. The share of market income from wages and other labor compensation rose and then fell for little net change, while the share of income from capital assets declined. Business income was the fastest growing source of income for the top 1 percent.

Because of the volatile nature of income from capital gains realizations and its significance for the highest-income households, it is more illuminating to look at sources of income as shares of market income excluding capital gains. Wages and other labor compensation rose from 40 percent of market income excluding capital gains in 1980 to close to 50 percent in 2000 and 2001 before dropping back to about 40 percent in 2007 (see Figure 10).

Capital income excluding capital gains—in other words, interest, dividends, and rents—has generally been a declining source of income among the highest-income households. Its share dropped from 42 percent of market income excluding capital gains in 1979 to 21 percent in 2002 and then increased to about 30 percent by 2007. Over the same period, the share of income from business activities grew sharply, increasing from a low of 10 percent of market income excluding capital gains in 1981 to a high of 27 percent in 2005 before dipping slightly in 2006 and 2007.

(Percentage of market income, excluding capital gains)

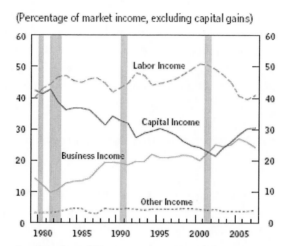

Source: Congressional Budget Office.

Note: For information on income definitions, the ranking of households, the allocation of taxes, and the construction of inequality indexes, see "Notes and Definitions" at the beginning of this study.

Figure 10. Shares of Market Income, by Source, for the Top 1 Percent of Households.

Capital gains are the most volatile source of income, and their importance as a share of household income for the top 1 percent of the population has fluctuated. That fluctuation appears to reflect movements in stock prices and changes in tax law.[23] Between 1979 and 1985, capital gains for the top 1 percent were equal to 20 percent to 30 percent of market income excluding capital gains; in 1986, they spiked to more than twice that share. The ratio of income from capital gains to other market income declined in the late 1980s and then began to pick up in the mid-1990s before entering a period of rapid growth starting in 1995. That ratio peaked at 35 percent of market income in 2000 before falling to 16 percent in 2002 and then rebounding to 37 percent in 2007.

The fall in capital income and the increase in business income may in part reflect a recharacterization of income. Following the Tax Reform Act of 1986, which lowered the top statutory tax rate on individual income below the top rate on corporate income, many C corporations (which are taxed separately from their owners under the corporate income tax) were converted to S corporations (which pass corporate income through to their shareholders, where it is taxed under the individual income tax). As a result, corporate dividend income and capital gains from the sale of corporate stock were converted into S corporation income, which is counted here as part of business income.

Business income jumped in the 1986– 1988 period as those conversions began, and it continued to grow rapidly throughout the 1990s and 2000s as more conversions occurred and new businesses were formed as S corporations rather than C corporations.

The changing composition of income for the highest-income households reflects a much longer trend. Over the entire 20th century, capital income declined sharply in importance for high-income taxpayers.[24] The labor share of income for the top income groups was higher in 2007 than before World War II, as highly compensated workers have replaced people whose income is from property or securities at the top of the income distribution.

What Explains the Rise in Income for the Top 1 Percent?

Rising labor income was a major component of the increase in income for the top 1 percent. A number of factors may have contributed to the rapid rise in earnings among the highest-income households. One potential explanation is that the compensation of "superstars" (such as actors, athletes, and musicians) may be especially sensitive to technological changes.[25] Unique characteristics of that labor market mean that technical innovations, such as cheap mass media, have made it possible for entertainers to reach much wider audiences. That increased exposure, in turn, has led to a manyfold increase in income for such people.

Another body of research has focused on the very large pay increases for top corporate executives.[26] Some researchers have argued that this growth in compensation can be accounted for by increases in firms' size. As firms grow larger and more complex, the impact on profits of corporate executives' decisions becomes greater, so firms may be more willing to pay large salaries to attract and keep the best executives. Other researchers have argued that weaknesses in corporate governance have enabled corporate executives to overpay themselves. Still others have focused on the form of compensation, arguing that the increasing importance of stock options in executive compensation has caused that compensation to grow rapidly during periods of rapid appreciation in the stock market.

Some researchers have attempted to evaluate the competing theories by dividing the highest earners into subgroups and by observing which subgroups saw the greatest increases in income. One study compiled the earnings in 2004 of the highest earners in various sectors of the economy on the basis of publicly available data, such as corporate annual reports and industry publications.[27] Using that approach, the authors were able to identify 9 percent of the taxpayers in the top 0.5 percent of the earnings spectrum. They found that corporate executives were a fairly small percentage of the highest earners, as were athletes and celebrities, and they did not grow in importance over the 1994–2004 period. In contrast, employees in the financial and legal professions made up a larger share of the highest earners than people in those other groups. The authors concluded that their findings are most consistent with the theories that technical changes have enhanced the value of certain skills and that the increasing scale of corporate and financial activity has raised the value of corporate executives and financial professionals, rather than that weak corporate governance has led to excessive compensation.

A similar study compiled data on the highest-income households on the basis of occupations reported on tax returns in the 1979–2005 period.[28] That study reached different conclusions. Its authors found that the rise in the highest-income households' share of income is explained by the prices of assets in financial markets and possibly by the evolution of corporate governance and entrepreneurship, rather than by superstar theories or by technological change that complemented certain skills. The study found that nonfinancial executives, managers, and supervisors made up the largest subgroup of the highest-income households, accounting for 31 percent of the top percentile. Medical professionals were the second largest occupational category, making up 16 percent, while financial professionals accounted for 14 percent and lawyers for 8 percent. No other single occupational group accounted for more than 5 percent of the top percentile. Some occupations have maintained steady shares of the top percentile over time, whereas others' shares have changed. Since 1979, nonfinancial executives saw their share decline a bit, from 36 percent to 31 percent. Within that group, the share attributable to salaried professionals declined sharply, while the share for executives of small businesses grew. The share of financial professionals almost doubled from 1979 to 2005. The study found that income growth was high for all the top-earning professions but varied substantially both within and across professions between those at the very highest part of the income scale and the rest of the top percentile. Executives, managers, supervisors, and financial professionals accounted for 60 percent of the increase in income accruing to the top percentile of the income distribution between 1979 and 2005.

Because of the important role of the financial sector, some researchers have focused on the pattern of compensation in that sector over a long period.[29] They found that the financial sector has become more complex since the 1980s and has thus needed more skilled labor. But even accounting for the education and skills of the workforce, the compensation differential between the financial sector and the rest of the economy appears inexplicably large from 1990 onward. The authors believe that deregulation and corporate finance activities linked to initial public offerings and credit risk are the primary causes of the higher compensation differential. However, because that particular study did not focus on the highest earners, it is not clear to what extent its findings can explain the rapid rise in income shares at the top of the distribution.

Others have argued that the observed growth in the conversion of C corporation income into S corporation income has contributed to the rapid growth in income for the highest-income households. That effect arises because such conversion can alter the timing of income. S corporations are required to pass all of their profits through to their shareholders in the year that they are earned, while C corporations face no such requirement. That phenomenon might be a contributing factor, but it can explain only a portion of the increase in the share of market income for the top 1 percent, much of which has come from increases in earnings.

The Effect of Government Transfer Payments and Federal Taxes

Even though an increasing concentration of market income was the primary force behind the growing dispersion in after-tax household income between 1979 and 2007, shifts in the distribution of government transfer payments and federal taxes also contributed to the increase in after-tax income inequality.[30]

Overall, transfers and federal taxes reduce income inequality. Transfers tend to make income more equal by boosting income for people at the bottom of the scale, and federal taxes tend to make income more equal because average tax rates (taxes as a percentage of household income) increase as income rises. In addition, the earned income tax credit, which in this analysis is included with federal taxes (though some of its benefits are conveyed in the form of government payments), has an effect on the income distribution similar to that of transfers by raising the after-tax income of lower-income households.

The effect of transfers and taxes on the dispersion of household income can be seen by comparing the Gini index for market income with the Gini index for after-transfer, before-tax income and the Gini index for after-transfer, after-federal-tax income. A proportional transfer and federal tax system would leave the Gini index for after-transfer, after-federal-tax income equal to that for market income. Transfers that are a decreasing percentage of market income as income rises (progressive transfers) lower the Gini index, as do federal taxes that are an increasing percentage of before-tax household income as income rises (progressive taxes). Because both transfers and federal taxes are progressive in the United States, they reduce the Gini index (see Figure 11). The dispersion of after-tax income in 2007 is about four-fifths as large as the dispersion of market income. Roughly 60 percent of the difference in dispersion between market income and after-tax income is attributable to transfers and roughly 40 percent is attributable to federal taxes.

The redistributive effect of transfers and federal taxes was smaller in 2007 than in 1979 (see Figure 12). In 1979, transfers and federal taxes reduced the Gini index from 0.479 to 0.367, a decrease of 11 percentage points (or 23 percent). In 2007, transfers and federal taxes reduced the Gini index from 0.590 to 0.489, a decline of 10 percentage points (or 17 percent). If transfers and federal taxes had had the same proportional equalizing effect in 2007 as they did in 1979, the Gini index for household income after transfers and federal taxes would have been 0.452 in 2007 instead of its actual value of 0.489.

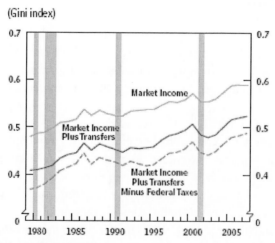

Source: Congressional Budget Office.
Note: For information on income definitions, the ranking of households, the allocation of taxes, and the construction of inequality indexes, see "Notes and Definitions" at the beginning of this study.

Figure 11. Summary Measures of Income Inequality, With and Without Transfers and Federal Taxes.

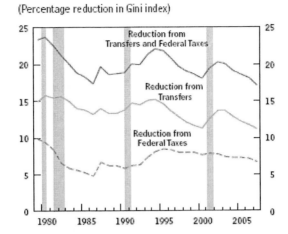

(Percentage reduction in Gini index)

Source: Congressional Budget Office.

Note: For information on income definitions, the ranking of households, the allocation of taxes, and the construction of inequality indexes, see "Notes and Definitions" at the beginning of this study.

Figure 12. Reduction in Income Inequality from Transfers and Federal Taxes.

Expressed in 2007 dollars, transfers and federal taxes reduced the average income difference between pairs of households in 1979 from $34,500 (twice 47.9 percent of market income) to $22,600 (twice 36.7 percent of income after transfers and federal taxes). In 2007, transfers and federal taxes reduced the average difference from $66,600 to $48,900. Those reductions occurred because income after transfers and federal taxes is more evenly distributed than market income and because it is smaller, on average.

As a result of the diminishing effect of transfers and federal taxes, the Gini index for income after transfers and federal taxes grew by more than the index for market income. Between 1979 and 2007, the Gini index for market income increased by 23 percent, the index for market income after transfers increased by 29 percent, and the index for income measured after transfers and federal taxes increased by 33 percent.

The equalizing effect of transfers and taxes depends on their degree of progressivity and on their size relative to household income. Holding the size of transfers and taxes constant, an increase in the progressivity of transfers and taxes will reduce income inequality. Holding the degree of progressivity constant, an increase in the size of transfers and taxes will also reduce inequality (assuming that both transfers and taxes are progressive).

The equalizing effect of transfers declined over the 1979–2007 period primarily because the distribution of transfers became less progressive. The equalizing effect of federal taxes also declined over the period, in part because the amount of federal taxes shrank as a share of market income and in part because of changes in the progressivity of the federal tax system.

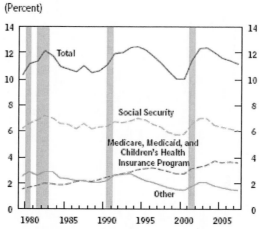

Source: Congressional Budget Office.
Note: For information on income definitions, the ranking of households, the allocation of taxes, and the construction of inequality indexes, see "Notes and Definitions" at the beginning of this study.

Figure 13. Transfers as a Percentage of Household Market Income.

Government Transfer Payments The amount of government transfer payments—including federal, state, and local transfers—relative to household market income was relatively constant from 1979 through 2007, ranging between 10 percent and 12 percent with no discernible trend (see Figure 13). Social Security benefits accounted for between 55 percent and 60 percent of the value of all transfers in each year of the period, equaling about 6½ percent of market income, on average. Even though average Social Security benefits grew more slowly than average income, the population receiving benefits grew faster than the overall population.

Medicare, Medicaid, and Children's Health Insurance Program benefits— measured here as their so-called fungible value—rose from under 2 percent to over 3 percent of market income.[31] Other transfers declined from nearly 3 percent of market income at their peak in 1982 to under 2 percent by 2007.[32] For transfer payments other than Social Security and unemployment insurance benefits, CBO relied on estimates of participation and benefit amounts from the Census Bureau's Current Population Survey.[33] Those payments are under-reported in the survey. Adjusting for underreporting to the extent possible would reduce the estimated inequality of after-transfer income but would have little effect on trends in inequality measured over long periods (see Box 3).

Effects of Transfers on Different Income Groups

The shifts in the relative importance of different transfer programs since 1979 moved the distribution of transfer benefits away from households in the lower part of the income spectrum to some extent (see Figure 14). Rapid growth in Medicare, which is not meanstested (in other words, not provided to people based on a test of need determined by their income and assets), tended to shift more transfer income to middle- and upper-income households. At the same time, spending on Aid to Families with Dependent Children and its successor, Temporary Assistance for Needy Families, has declined relative to market income; benefits from those means-tested programs are heavily con-centrated at the bottom of the income scale. As a result, households in the lowest-income quintile received 54 percent of federal transfer payments in 1979 and 36 percent in 2007.

As a consequence of those shifts, the redistributive effect of transfers has changed over time and changed in different ways for subgroups of the population. Largely because of the decrease in the share of transfers accruing to households in the lower part of the income scale, the overall redistributive effect of transfers lessened between 1979 and 2007 (see Figure 12). That decline was irregular, though, as the effect of transfers increased in periods in which transfer income grew more quickly than market income (such as the recessions of 1990–1991 and 2001) and decreased in periods in which transfer income grew more slowly than market income.

Effects of Transfers on Different Types of Households

Because outlays on programs focused on the older population (such as Social Security and Medicare) have grown faster than outlays on other transfer programs, the share of transfers received by elderly childless households has likewise increased, while the portion going to households with children has declined. Elderly households received 62 percent of total transfers in 1979 and 68 percent in 2007 (see Figure 15). Households with children received a much smaller and declining share of transfers—19 percent in 1979 and 12 percent in 2007.[34] Nonelderly childless households saw the smallest fluctuations in their share of transfers, which ranged between 17 percent and 21 percent over the period. The most significant sources of cash transfers for nonelderly childless households are Social Security disability benefits and retirement benefits for early retirees (those who retire between age 62 and age 65), unemployment insurance benefits, and workers' compensation. Some of those households also receive health insurance through Medicare or Medicaid.

Transfers have a large redistributive effect for elderly childless households because those households receive a large share of transfers and because they have belowaverage market income. Over the 1979–2007 period, transfers ranged from 45 percent to 60 percent of market income for the elderly. Those transfers reduced income inequality (measured by the Gini index) among elderly households by between 25 percent and 35 percent during that period (see Figure 16). The redistributive effect of transfers for those households fluctuated throughout the period, largely reflecting changes in the size of transfers relative to other income. There has been a trend toward a smaller share of transfer payments that accrue to elderly households accruing to the low-income elderly, lessening the redistributive effect over the period.

The effect of transfers on income inequality is much smaller for households with children and nonelderly childless households. For those groups, transfers equaled between 4 percent and 6 percent of market income. Early in the 1979–2007 period, transfers had a larger redistributive effect on households with children, but that effect diminished in the mid- to late 1990s to the level experienced by nonelderly childless households. That convergence occurred because transfers as a share of income decreased for households with children and because the share of those payments accruing to lower income households fell.35 For both groups, the redistributive effect of transfers rose in years near the 1990–1991 and 2001 recessions, when transfer payments grew faster than market income.

Box 3. The Misreporting of Transfer Income

In its measure of transfer income, the Congressional Budget Office (CBO) includes payments from most government transfer programs: Social Security, Medicare, Medicaid, the Supplemental Nutrition Assistance Program (SNAP, formerly called the Food Stamp program), Supplemental Security Income (SSI), Temporary Assistance for Needy Families (TANF, and its predecessor, Aid to Families with Dependent Children, AFDC), unemployment insurance, and state and local government cash transfers, as well as housing subsidies, energy assistance, and free or reduced-price school breakfasts and lunches.

Those sources of income are quite important for many low-income households. Tax returns contain little information about transfer income because most of it is not taxed. For Social Security and unemployment insurance benefits, which are partially taxable, CBO uses information from tax returns together with information from the Current Population Survey (CPS). CBO's estimates of income from those sources generally exceed 90 percent of the amount that the government agencies that administer the programs report paying in benefits. For transfer payments other than Social Security and unemployment insurance be-nefits, CBO relies on estimates of participation and benefit amounts from the CPS. Unfortunately, the shares of different types of transfer payments that are reported in the CPS are relatively low, and they have generally been declining over time. A recent study found that the share of Food Stamp benefit dollars captured in the CPS declined from 67 percent in 1993 to 55 percent in 2005.[1] For AFDC and TANF, reporting rates declined from 75 percent in 1993 to 57 percent in 2005. In con-trast, reporting of SSI benefits rose from 76 percent to 82 percent over the same period.

To analyze how the misreporting of transfer income might affect estimates of the income distribution, CBO tabulated data from the Transfer Income Model (TRIM3).[2]

That model corrects for the misreporting of transfer income by applying the rules of several transfer programs to each household in the CPS to determine if households are eligible for benefits and, if so, the size of the benefit they can receive.

Households that report receiving benefits, and who appear to be eligible, are assigned the computed amount of the benefit. Households that report receiving benefits but who appear to be ineligible are assumed to receive no benefits. For households that do not report receiving benefits but who appear to be eligible, new participants are created in such a way as to match the number and characteristics of recipients reported in government agencies' program data. The model targets the number of recipients rather than the overall amount of benefits, but the estimated benefit amounts approximate the agencies' totals.

To assess the sensitivity of its main analysis to the misreporting of transfers, CBO combined estimates of transfer payments from TRIM3 with its own merged data from tax returns and the CPS. For the programs covered by TRIM3—Food Stamps, SSI, TANF/AFDC, and housing subsidies—CBO replaced benefits as reported in the CPS with benefits as estimated using TRIM3. CBO then recalculateed income, reranked households according to their corrected income, and tabulated new estimates of the distribution of income. CBO did that analysis for 1993 and 2004, the earliest and latest years for which TRIM3 estimates are available.

Underreporting of transfer income increased between 1993 and 2004. However, transfer income increased more slowly than market income over that period. As a result, the reporting adjustments were larger in 2004 than in 1993 as a share of transfer income, but smaller as a share of total household income. Therefore, the reporting adjustments had a smaller effect on the Gini index in 2004 than in 1993.

Adjusting for the misreporting of transfer payments adds income for households at the bottom of the distribution of income. Conse-quently, the Gini index adjusted for misreporting is lower than the unadjusted Gini index. For 1993, reporting adjustments cause the Gini index to fall from 0.455 to 0.450, or by about 1 percent; for 2004, reporting adjustments lower the Gini index from 0.502 to 0.498, or by 0.8 percent.

[1]. Laura Wheaton, "Underreporting of Means-Tested Transfer Programs in the CPS and SIPP," 2007 Proceedings of the American Statistical Association, Social Statistics Section [CDROM] (Alexandria, Va.: American Statistical Association, 2007), pp. 3622–3629.

[2]. The model was developed and is maintained by the Urban Institute, with funding primarily from the Department of Health and Human Services, Office of the Assistant Secretary for Planning and Evaluation. TRIM3 requires users to input assumptions and interpretations about economic behavior and the rules governing federal programs. Therefore, the conclusions presented here are attributable only to CBO.

Federal Taxes

Changes in the effect of taxes on the distribution of aftertax income can come about because of a change in the overall average tax rate, a change in the composition of taxes, or changes in the progressivity of particular taxes.

Over the 1979–2007 period:

- The overall average federal tax rate (combined federal taxes as a share of household income including transfers) fell by a small amount,
- The composition of federal revenues shifted away from income taxes to payroll taxes (which are less progressive),

- The federal individual income tax became slightly more progressive, and
- The payroll tax became slightly less progressive.

On balance, those factors reduced the extent to which federal taxes lessened the degree of income inequality.36 As a result, the increase in inequality of after-tax incomewas greater than the increase in inequality of before-tax income.

A Lower Average Federal Tax Rate

The overall average federal tax rate dropped from 22 percent in 1979 to 20 percent in 2007 (see Figure 17). The average tax rate declined in the early 1980s, then rose through much of the 1980s and 1990s. It peaked at 23 percent in 2000, and then fell sharply following the 2001 recession and tax legislation enacted in 2001 and 2003, reaching just under 20 percent in 2003, the lowest rate since 1979. By 2007, the overall rate had risen to just above 20 percent, a percentage point below the average for the 29-year period.

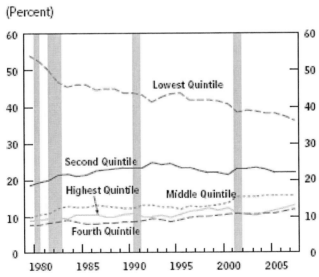

Source: Congressional Budget Office.

Note: For information on income definitions, the ranking of households, the allocation of taxes, and the construction of inequality indexes, see "Notes and Definitions" at the beginning of this study.

Figure 14. Share of Total Transfers, by Market Income Group.

(Percent)

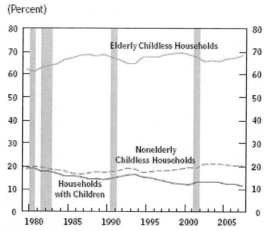

Source: Congressional Budget Office.

Note: For information on income definitions, the ranking of households, the allocation of taxes, and the construction of inequality indexes, see "Notes and Definitions" at the beginning of this study.

Figure 15. Share of Total Transfers, by Type of Household.

A Shift from Income Taxes to Payroll Taxes

The composition of federal taxes changed between 1979 and 2007, as payroll taxes grew faster than income taxes. The average payroll tax rate (social insurance taxes as a percentageof household income including transfers) was slightly higher in 2007 than it was in 1979, but the average individual income tax rate was slightly lower. Those variations stemmed from a combination of legislative changes and economic developments.

The increase in the payroll tax rate in the 1980s resulted from legislated increases in the cap on earnings subject to the Social Security payroll tax and from legislation enacted in 1983 that accelerated previously scheduled increases in the Social Security payroll tax rate. Subsequent legislation in the early 1990s first increased and then eliminated the cap on earnings subject to the Hospital Insurance payroll tax (which is used to finance aportion of Medicare). The payroll tax rate declined in the late 1990s and early 2000s as labor income grew more slowly than other income sources and as earnings above the maximum level subject to Social Security taxes grew more rapidly than earnings below that level.

The average individual income tax rate peaked at 12 percent of household income in 1981. That rate then fell as the reduction in tax rates enacted in 1981 took effect.

The average individual income tax rate rose again in the late 1990s because of legislation enacted in 1993 and because of rapidly rising incomes. After 2000, the rate fell once more as a result of the 2001 and 2003 tax cuts and the recession in 2001.

An Increase in the Progressivity of Federal Individual Income Taxes. Virtually all of the progressivity of the federal tax system derives from the individual income tax.

Average federal income tax rates in 2007 ranged from -5.6 percent for households in the lowest income quintile to 18.8 percent for the 1 percent of the population with the highest income (see the top panel of Figure 18). The lowest income quintile has a negative average federal tax rate because, as a group, households in that quintile qualify for more in refundable tax credits than they owe in income taxes before the credits are applied. Average federal income tax rates were lower in 2007 than in 1979 across the income distribution. The pattern in the intervening years is more varied, reflecting the interaction of numerous changes to tax law and changes in the composition and distribution of income.

After rising between 1979 and 1983, average federal individual income tax rates declined almost continuously thereafter for the 60 percent of the population in the three middle income quintiles. For example, the income tax rate for the middle quintile declined from approximately 8 percent in 1981 to about 3 percent in 2003 and remained at about that level through 2007.

The rapid decline in the rates between 2000 and 2003 reflects numerous changes in law enacted in 2001—such as the expansion of the child tax credit, reductions in tax rates, and reductions in the income tax burden on married couples—that lessened taxes for households in the middle quintiles. The decline in the average federal individual income tax rate since 1979 was largest for those in the lowest income quintile, primarily because of increases in the earned income tax credit.

The average federal income tax rate for the 1 percent of the population with the highest income fell in the early 1980s and then rose following enactment of the Tax Reform Act of 1986. The average tax rate for that group then fell somewhat again in the latter half of the 1980s before climbing in the 1990s. That increase reflected changes in law that raised tax rates for that group as well as rapid increases in their income, which caused their average tax rate to rise as more income was taxed in higher tax brackets. Tax rates for the highest-income households declined after 2000.

(Percentage reduction in the Gini index)

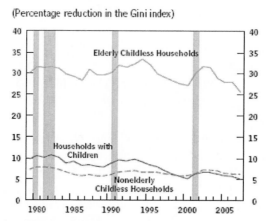

Source: Congressional Budget Office.

Note: For information on income definitions, the ranking of households, the allocation of taxes, and the construction of inequality indexes, see "Notes and Definitions" at the beginning of this study.

Figure 16. Reduction in Income Inequality from Transfers for Different Types of Households.

(Percent)

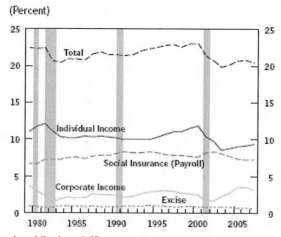

Source: Congressional Budget Office.

Note: For information on income definitions, the ranking of households, the allocation of taxes, and the construction of inequality indexes, see "Notes and Definitions" at the beginning of this study.

Figure 17. Federal Taxes as a Percentage of Household Income Including Transfers.

(Percent)

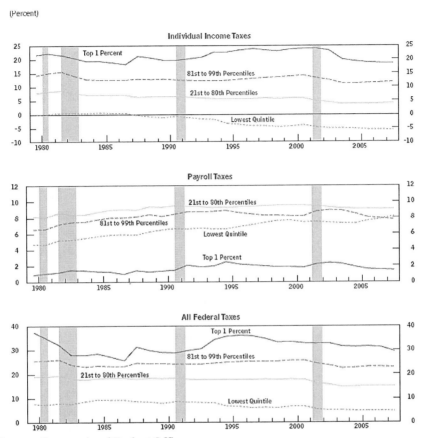

Source: Congressional Budget Office.

Note: For information on income definitions, the ranking of households, the allocation of taxes, and the construction of inequality indexes, see "Notes and Definitions" at the beginning of this study.

Figure 18. Federal Taxes as a Percentage of Household Income, by Income Group.

The decline was especially rapid in 2003, when a reduction in the tax rate for the top tax bracket enacted in 2001 took effect and further changes in law reduced tax rates on dividends and realized capital gains.

To measure the level and change over time in the progressivity of taxes, researchers have developed various approaches to summarizing the distribution of taxes into a single number. One such approach compares the Gini indexes for before-tax and after-tax income, essentially defining progressivity as the degree to which taxes equalize the distribution of income (see Appendix B). A Gini index for after-tax income that is smaller than the corresponding index for before-tax income indicates that the distribution of after-tax income is more equal than the distribution of before-tax income; a larger index for after-tax income than before-tax income indicates the opposite. Under this approach, the federal individual income tax was slightly more progressive in 2007 than in 1979; that tax became more progressive between 1990 and 2000 and less progressive after 2001 (see the top panel of Figure 19).

An alternative measure of progressivity compares the share of taxes with the share of income for households ranked by income. That index effectively defines progressivity as the degree to which tax payments are more concentrated than income. (A measure that only compared the shares of taxes paid across households would be an inappropriate indicator of tax pro-gressivity because it would not account for the shares of income across households.)

By that measure of tax concentration, the federal individual income tax was notably more progressive in 2007 than in 1979; it became more progressi-ve from 1990 through 1995 and again between 2000 and 2003, and it became slightly less progressive after 2003 (see the bottom panel of Figure 19).

A Decrease in the Progressivity of Payroll Taxes. In contrast to federal individual income taxes, which are progressive over the full range of household incomes, payroll taxes are not. In 2007, payroll taxes as a share of household income ranged from 8 percent for the lowest quintile to about 9 percent for other income groups up through the 80th percentile (see the middle panel of Figure 18). Average payroll tax rates were lower for higher income groups, dropping to under 2 percent for the highest income percentile. The average rate was lower for higher income households because a large portion of their earnings were above the maximum taxable amount for Social Security payroll taxes and because a larger fraction of their household income was not from earnings and thus not subject to payroll taxes.[37]

The average payroll tax rate rose for all income groups from 1979 through the end of the 1980s as a result of legislated increases in the tax rate and expansions in the tax base. The rate rose again for the lowest income quintile after 1993, reflecting an increased share of income from wages for that group. The payroll tax rate also rose in the early 1990s for the highest-earning taxpayers following legislated increases to the maximum taxable amount for Hospital Insurance payroll taxes, but that rate fell thereafter as total income for those taxpayers grew more rapidly than the maximum taxable amount for Social Security.

Both approaches to measuring tax progressivity indicate that payroll taxes are regressive overall. The measure that compares shares of taxes with shares of income is negative, indicating that higher-income households pay a smaller share of payroll taxes than their share of income.

The measure that compares the Gini indexes for beforetax and after-tax income is also negative, indicating that income after payroll taxes is more unequally distributed than income before payroll taxes. Both measures have become more negative over time, indicating that payroll taxes have become more regressive over the 1979–2007 period. That change occurred because payroll tax rates rose the most for households at the bottom of the income distribution, as their labor income grew more rapidly than their other sources of income over the period.

The Change in the Overall Progressivity of the Federal Tax System. Taken as a whole, the federal tax system is progressive. In 2007, total federal tax rates ranged from under 5 percent of income for households in the bottom quintile to 14 percent for households in the middle quintiles to just under 30 percent for households in the highest income percentile (see the bottom panel of Figure 18).[38] From the mid-1980s through the mid-1990s, tax rates rose for the top quintile but fell for the lowest income quintile. Rates for all income groups declined from 2000 through 2007.

Because tax rates were lower for all income groups in 2007 than in 1979, it is not immediately apparent from examining tax rates alone whether combined federal taxes became more or less progressive over that period. By the progressivity measure that compares the Gini indexes for before-tax and after-tax income, the federal tax system as a whole was slightly less progressive in 2007 than in 1979 (see the top panel of Figure 19). By that measure, combined federal taxes became much less progressive in the first part of the 1980s, much more progressive in the first part of the 1990s, and slightly less progressive since then.

By the alternative measure of tax concentration (discussed above) that compares shares of taxes with shares of income, the federal tax system as a whole was about as progressive in 2007 as it was in 1979 (see the bottom panel of Figure 19).39 Combined federal taxes became slightly less progressive in the early 1980s and slightly more progressive in the early 1990s and have been mostly unchanged since then.

The difference in estimated changes in progressivity reflects different concepts of progressivity. Although federal tax payments were about as concentrated relative to the concentration of income in 2007 as in 1979, the equalizing effect of federal taxes on household income was smaller. That result reflects the decrease in the average tax rate over the period. If federal taxes had represented the same share of household income in 2007 as they did in 1979, the similar concentration of tax payments would have implied a similar equalizing effect.

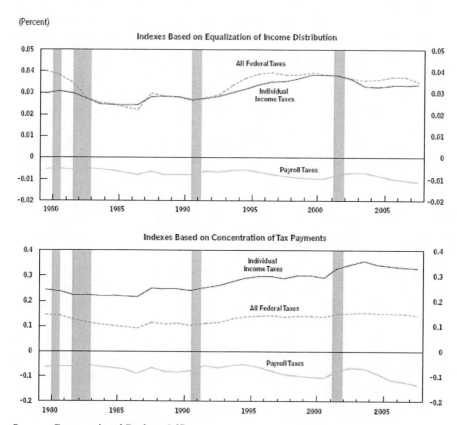

Figure 19. Indexes of the Progressivity of Federal Taxes.

Source: Congressional Budget Office.
Notes: For information on income definitions, the ranking of households, the allocation of taxes, and the construction of inequality indexes, see "Notes and Definitions" at the beginning of this study. The indexes in the top panel are calculated as the difference between the Gini indexes for income before and after federal taxes. The indexes in the bottom panel are based on a comparison of shares of federal taxes with shares of income for households ranked by income.

Federal Taxes on Different Types of Households

The impact of the federal tax system varies across types of households. Some differences arise because several provisions of federal tax law explicitly provide benefits to certain types of households. For example, the child tax credit, exemptions for dependents, head of household filing status, and the earned income tax credit all reduce tax burdens on households with children relative to those without children. Other differences arise because income from various sources is more or less significant for different types of households and is taxed at different rates. For example, payroll taxes apply only to earnings (and thus are quite important to nonelderly households), whereas special tax rules apply to income from Social Security, capital gains, and dividends (and are relatively more important to elderly households, for whom those sources represent a larger share of their income). Other differences arise because of the interaction between the distribution of income and the progressive nature of the federal tax system.

Even though elderly childless households have a lower average federal tax rate than any other group, federal taxes have a greater redistributive effect on them than on other types of households (see Figure 20). Because earnings are a relatively small source of income for elderly households, payroll tax burdens, which tend to be regressive, are low.

In contrast, capital income is a more important source of income for elderly households, and federal taxes on capital income and the portion of the federal corporate tax attributed to elderly households, which are very pro-gressive under the assumption that owners of capital bear the economic burden of corporate income taxes, are relatively high.

The redistributive effect of taxes on elderly households dropped sharply during the first five years of the time period studied here. That change was primarily driven by a decline in federal corporate income tax payments. After some variation in the interim, that effect was about the same in 2007 as it was in 1983.

For households with children, the redistributive effect of federal taxes in 2007 was almost as large as for elderly households. That progressivity derives almost exclusively from the federal individual income tax, which is most redistributive for households with children. In addition to the progressive rate structure of the tax code, the earned income tax credit and the child tax credit are very progressive, mainly benefiting low- and moderate-income households with children. Because of those credits (and the structure of tax rates), households with children in the lowest 40 percent of the overall income distribution receive more in refundable tax credits than they otherwise owe in federal income taxes, and households with children in the middle fifth of the distribution pay less than 2 percent of their income in federal individual income taxes.

The redistributive effect of federal taxes declined for households with children in the first years of the 1979–2007 period as payroll taxes rose while federal individual and corporate income taxes fell. The redistributive effect rose throughout the 1990s as a series of changes to tax law increased the concentration of federal tax payments among higher-income households. Rate increases for high-income taxpayers coupled with an expansion of the earned income tax credit and creation of the child tax credit caused the average federal individual income tax rate to decrease at the bottom of the distribution while increasing at the top. Additionally, as income rose rapidly at the top of the distribution, federal income taxes paid by those taxpayers climbed even more rapidly because of the progressive nature of the tax system. After the late 1990s, the redistributive effect of federal taxes on households with children changed little. Although the concentration of federal income tax payments continued to rise, that effect was offset by a general decline in federal taxes as a share of income.

Over most of the 29-year period, the federal tax system was least redistributive for nonelderly childless households.

Those households face a similar mix of taxes as households with children, but they face a less progressive federal income tax system.

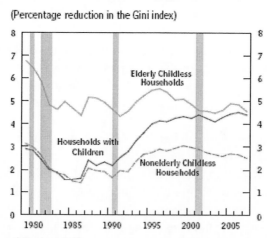

(Percentage reduction in the Gini index)

Source: Congressional Budget Office.

Note: For information on income definitions, the ranking of households, the allocation of taxes, and the construction of inequality indexes, see "Notes and Definitions" at the beginning of this study.

Figure 20. Indexes of Federal Tax Progressivity Based on Equalization of Income Distribution for Different Types of Households.

In the early years of the period, the redistributive effect of federal taxes on nonelderly childless households was almost identical to the effect on households with children. However, the increases in the concentration of federal tax payments were not nearly as large in the 1990s for this group as for households with children, because low-income childless households did not receive new tax benefits of the same magnitude as low-income households with children. In the 2000s, the redistributive effect of federal taxes on non-elderly childless households declined slightly. The concentration of federal tax payments for such households was little changed, but federal taxes claimed a smaller share of income, causing the redistributive effect of federal taxation to decline.

APPENDIX A: MEASURING HOUSEHOLD INCOME

This appendix explains the data and the assumptions used in this Congressional Budget Office (CBO) analysis.

Sources of Data

This analysis draws its information on income from two primary sources. The core data come from the Statistics of Income (SOI), a nationally representative sample of individual income tax returns collected by the Internal Revenue Service (IRS). The number of returns sampled grew over the time period studied, ranging from roughly 90,000 in some of the early years to more than 300,000 in the later years. CBO used the full Individual Income Tax file, which contains more detail than the public-use version of the file released by the IRS. CBO supplemented that information with data from the Annual Social and Economic Supplement to the Census Bureau's Current Population Survey (CPS), which contains survey data on the demographic characteristics and income of a large sample of households.

One limitation of the data is that both the SOI and the CPS lack important information needed for estimating and comparing after-tax household income over time. The SOI lacks information on couples and individuals who do not file a federal tax return, does not report all income from government cash transfer programs, has no information on the receipt of in-kind transfers and benefits, and uses tax returns rather than households as the reporting unit. The CPS lacks detailed information on high-income households, does not report capital gains, underreports other income from capital, and lacks information on deductions and adjustments necessary to compute taxes.

To overcome the limitations of the two data sources, CBO statistically matched each SOI record to a corresponding CPS record on the basis of demographic characteristics and income. Each pairing resulted in a new record that took on the demographic characteristics of the CPS record and the income reported in the SOI. Some types of income, such as certain transfer payments and in-kind benefits, appear only in the CPS; values for those items were drawn directly from that survey. Because not all households have to file tax returns, some households do not appear in the SOI; thus, the CPS reflects more households. After all SOI records were matched to CPS records, the remaining survey records were recorded as households that did not file an income tax return, and their income values were taken directly from the CPS. CBO then estimated the tax liability for each matched record.

Measuring Income

CBO constructed three measures of household income for this analysis:

- The first measure—*before-transfer, before-tax household income* (called market income in this study)—includes all cash income (both taxable and tax-exempt), taxes paid by businesses (which are imputed to households as described below), and the value of income received in-kind from sources such as employer-paid health insurance premiums. The taxes paid by businesses are the imputed value of corporate income taxes (which are considered to be part of capital income) and the employer's share of payroll taxes (which are considered to be part of labor income). They are included in the measure under the assumption that household income would have been higher by a corresponding amount in the absence of those taxes.

- The second measure—*after-transfer, before-tax house-hold income*— adds cash transfer payments (such as Social Security, unemployment insurance, and welfare benefits) to market income, along with estimates of the value of in-kind benefits (from Medicare, Medic aid, the Children's Health Insurance Program (CHIP), the Supplemental Nutrition Assistance Program (formerly known as the Food Stamp program), and other programs).

- The third measure—*after-transfer, after-federal-tax household income* (called after-tax income in this study)—subtracts federal individual and corporate income taxes, social insurance (payroll) taxes, and excise taxes. In this analysis, CBO did not subtract other federal taxes (such as estate and gift taxes) or state and local taxes in constructing after-tax income.

CBO used the Census Bureau's measure of so-called fungible value to determine the cash equivalent of in-kind government transfer payments. Fungible value is an estimate of the value to recipients of benefits received in kind. Some benefits are assessed at market value— the cost recipients would incur if they bought the goods themselves. The value assigned to food stamps, for example, equals their face value, and school meals are counted as the subsidy cost borne by the government.

The value of other in-kind benefits, such as benefits paid by Medicare, Medicaid, and CHIP, equals the amount of households' resources freed up for other uses by the health care services provided, up to the average cost (total cost to the government divided by the number of program participants) of those services. Placing an appropriate value on medical insurance is difficult, however.[1] (For an extended discussion of that issue, see Appendix C.)

Adjusting Income for Differences among Households

CBO used households as the unit of analysis. A household includes all people living in a single housing unit. The presumption is that households make joint economic decisions, which may not be true in every case (in a group house, for example). Households may comprise more than one taxpaying unit, such as a married couple and their adult children living together.

Households with identical income may differ in ways that bear on their economic status. Importantly, larger households need more income than smaller households to achieve the same economic status. At the same time, economies of scale in at least some types of consumption—housing, in particular—mean that two people do not need twice the income to live as well as an individual living alone. As a result, assessing economic status on the basis of per capita income (total household income divided by household size) ignores the benefits of shared consumption. An adjusted measure of income falling somewhere between household income and per capita income is likely to offer a better perspective on economic status. In this study, CBO adjusted for household size by dividing household income by an adjustment factor

equal to the square root of the number of people in the household, counting
adults and children equally. That adjustment implies that each additional
person increases a household's needs but at a decreasing rate.[2]

It may also be desirable to adjust the income of households for other
differences in their circumstances that affect their economic position. For
example, the prices of goods and services vary among locations, and households can incur different costs associated with working, such as the costs of
commuting and child care expenses, depending on how many members are
employed. In this analysis, CBO did not adjust for those additional differences
among households.

Income Categories

In this analysis, CBO presents data on income and taxes for various
subgroups of the population, such as the lowest 20 percent or the top 1 percent.
In constructing those subgroups, households are ranked by income that is
adjusted for household size. Each subgroup of the population contains an equal
number of people, but because households vary in size, subgroups generally
contain unequal numbers of households.

Incidence of Federal Taxes

CBO assumed that households bear the economic cost of the taxes they
pay directly, such as individual income taxes and the employee's share of
payroll taxes. CBO further assumed—as do most economists—that the
employer's share of payroll taxes is passed on to employees in the form of
lower wages than would otherwise be paid.

Therefore, CBO included the amount of those taxes in labor income and
counted the taxes as part of household taxes.

CBO also assumed that the economic costs of excise taxes fall on
households according to their consumption of taxed goods (such as tobacco
and alcohol). Excise taxes on intermediate goods, which are paid by
businesses, were attributed to households in proportion to their overall
consumption. CBO assumed that each household spends the same amount on
taxed goods as a similar household with comparable income in the Bureau of
Labor Statistics' Consumer Expenditure Survey.

Table A-1. Income Category Minimums, 1979 to 2007
(2007 dollars)

Year	Lowest Quintile	Second Quintile	Middle Quintile	Fourth Quintile	81st-90th Percentiles	91st-95th Percentiles	96th-99th Percentiles	Top 1 Percent
			Market Income Plus Transfers					
1979	0	12,823	25,095	36,165	51,289	66,177	84,243	165,049
1980	0	11,679	23,884	34,837	49,952	65,052	82,035	160,192
1981	0	11,576	23,775	34,962	50,269	64,931	82,417	157,184
1982	0	10,942	22,676	34,161	49,966	65,043	81,463	157,152
1983	0	10,588	22,368	34,124	50,333	66,092	83,946	164,076
1984	0	11,575	23,811	35,804	52,660	69,339	88,492	176,324
1985	0	11,731	23,996	36,388	53,439	70,645	90,614	182,408
1986	0	11,674	24,431	37,502	55,851	73,994	96,189	211,734
1987	0	10,917	24,247	37,880	56,609	75,078	96,583	198,913
1988	0	11,269	24,935	38,524	57,719	76,637	99,333	214,137
1989	0	11,643	25,273	39,082	58,173	77,769	101,227	217,203
1990	0	12,022	25,198	38,384	57,464	76,458	99,457	207,178
1991	0	11,591	24,259	37,979	56,428	75,209	97,958	203,670
1992	0	11,028	24,098	38,111	57,027	76,416	100,258	215,111
1993	0	11,013	23,939	38,046	57,398	76,678	100,620	211,008
1994	0	11,183	24,341	38,952	58,474	78,114	102,425	218,209
1995	0	12,218	25,307	39,612	59,901	80,381	106,301	230,851
1996	0	12,181	25,445	40,083	60,965	82,462	109,621	244,785
1997	0	12,716	26,091	40,942	62,189	85,783	115,270	259,427

Year	Lowest Quintile	Second Quintile	Middle Quintile	Fourth Quintile	81st-90th Percentiles	91st-95th Percentiles	96th-99th Percentiles	Top 1 Percent
1998	0	13,780	27,130	42,515	64,940	88,854	120,428	277,770
1999	0	14,258	27,836	43,578	66,755	91,542	123,864	296,430
2000	0	13,930	27,539	43,729	67,308	93,072	127,167	304,593
2001	0	13,563	27,273	43,003	66,512	90,969	122,144	274,135
2002	0	12,992	26,145	41,757	64,760	88,819	118,862	259,846
2003	0	12,536	25,934	41,896	65,567	89,789	120,573	265,390
2004	0	12,847	26,727	42,855	67,083	92,368	124,797	288,190
2005	0	13,415	26,993	43,464	68,025	95,001	131,128	322,859
2006	0	13,563	27,215	44,070	69,314	96,786	133,961	337,634
2007	0	14,851	28,618	45,192	70,578	98,955	137,578	347,421
Market Income Plus Transfers Minus Federal Taxes								
1979	0	17,394	27,563	37,861	52,803	67,496	85,634	167,365
1980	0	16,705	26,678	36,781	51,554	66,629	83,706	162,320
1981	0	16,473	26,487	36,988	51,982	66,629	84,379	159,784
1982	0	15,988	25,825	36,465	51,956	66,987	83,800	160,358
1983	0	15,295	25,557	36,462	52,283	67,737	85,748	167,000
1984	0	16,229	26,665	38,092	54,437	71,307	90,473	178,821
1985	0	16,304	27,093	38,689	55,204	72,538	92,686	185,834
1986	0	16,492	27,860	39,931	57,618	75,888	98,436	215,506
1987	0	15,897	27,719	40,223	58,387	76,969	98,368	202,586
1988	0	16,332	28,347	41,006	59,510	78,824	101,171	217,957
1989	0	16,720	28,774	41,448	60,316	79,959	103,537	220,654

Year	Lowest Quintile	Second Quintile	Middle Quintile	Fourth Quintile	81st-90th Percentiles	91st-95th Percentiles	96th-99th Percentiles	Top 1 Percent
1990	0	17,116	28,809	41,199	59,485	78,614	101,968	210,743
1991	0	17,055	28,286	40,786	58,597	77,401	100,232	206,690
1992	0	16,667	28,369	41,135	59,323	78,808	103,311	218,623
1993	0	16,899	28,483	41,075	59,840	79,225	103,024	215,061
1994	0	17,077	28,896	42,051	60,718	80,455	105,247	221,474
1995	0	17,916	29,893	42,762	62,352	83,317	109,400	235,420
1996	0	17,622	30,179	43,391	63,557	85,572	112,829	248,706
1997	0	18,076	30,591	44,069	65,054	88,139	118,285	263,875
1998	0	18,918	31,736	45,626	67,561	91,954	123,395	281,724
1999	0	19,402	32,444	46,610	69,545	94,613	127,211	300,386
2000	0	19,030	32,219	46,880	70,279	96,330	130,399	308,989
2001	0	19,204	32,352	47,091	69,709	93,970	125,600	278,582
2002	0	18,745	31,526	46,069	68,029	91,974	122,069	265,040
2003	0	18,461	31,317	46,034	68,999	92,732	123,655	269,239
2004	0	18,852	32,089	47,331	70,639	95,934	128,279	293,352
2005	0	19,092	32,632	48,109	71,740	98,573	135,153	327,829
2006	0	19,466	32,999	48,760	73,172	100,851	138,171	341,717
2007	0	20,448	34,261	49,960	74,732	102,918	141,914	352,875

Source: Congressional Budget Office.

Note: For information on income definitions, the ranking of households, the allocation of taxes, and the construction of inequality indexes, see "Notes and Definitions" at the beginning of this study. For each of the years 1979 through 2007, Table A-1 presents the range of income in each income category for the three income definitions that CBO uses in the study: market income, market income plus government transfers, and market income plus government transfers minus federal taxes.

In this analysis, CBO assumed that owners of capital bear the economic burden of corporate income taxes in proportion to their income from capital, measured as interest, dividends, rents, and adjusted capital gains.

Adjusted capital gains—capital gains scaled to their longterm historical level given the size of the economy and the tax rate that applies to them—were used in place of actual realizations in allocating corporate income taxes so as to smooth out large year-to-year variations in the amount of gains.

The incidence of the corporate income tax is uncertain.

In the very short term, owners of corporate equity are likely to bear most of the economic burden of the tax; but over the longer term, as capital markets adjust, the economic burden of the tax is spread across owners of all types of capital. Moreover, the burden will fall partly on wage earners to the extent that domestic investment declines as capital shifts to other countries or domestic saving falls because of the tax, thereby lowering the growth in workers' productivity and wages. For this analysis, however, CBO assumed that the economic burden of the corporate income tax is spread proportionately across all forms of capital income.[3]

State and Local Taxes

CBO did not include state and local taxes in this analysis because of the difficulty of estimating them for individual households over a long period. State sales taxes would be particularly challenging, as no major survey collects data on sales taxes paid by households. It is unclear how the omission of those taxes affects conclusions about trends in the redistributive effect of the entire tax system.

Between 1979 and 2007, state and local taxes ranged between 8.2 percent and 9.3 percent of gross domestic product—equal to about 40 percent to 50 percent of federal taxes. State and local taxes have three primary components, and the composition of receipts has been fairly stable over time. Sales taxes are the largest source, accounting for 34 percent of state and local tax revenue in 2007. Those taxes are generally assumed to be roughly proportional to consumption, making the tax regressive with respect to income (because lower-income households consume a greater proportion of their income than do higher-income households). Property taxes accounted for 30 percent of state and local tax revenue in 2007. The progressivity of those taxes depends critically on their incidence, which is a matter of considerable debate. State individual income taxes, which accounted for 22 percent of state and local tax revenues in 2007, are much less progressive than the federal individual income tax because the rate structures for state-level income taxes are flatter than those at the federal level and any refundable credits are small. Thus, although different analysts have reached different conclusions about whether state and local taxes on net are proportional, progressive, or regressive, they are clearly less progressive than the federal tax system. Consequently, analysis of the entire tax system would show less progressivity than analysis of the federal tax system alone. However, it is more difficult to know how changes in state and local taxes over time have affected trends in tax progressivity.[4]

Limitations of Using Annual Data This study presents a series of annual snapshots of household income from 1979 through 2007. Because the data represent the experiences of different people in each year, the analysis does not provide information about changes in the income of a particular household or a group of households over multiyear periods.

That approach has two significant limitations. First, the year-to-year variation in income means that a household's distributional rank based on annual income may not accurately represent its economic resources; for example, a household in one of the lower income quintiles in a particular year may have assets that make it relatively well off. A household's consumption derives less from its current income than from the normal, or permanent, income the household expects to have over time. People may rely on savings or borrowing to tide themselves over during periods of unemployment, for example.

A second, and related, limitation is that some forms of income come irregularly, particularly capital gains from the sale of a business, shares of stock, or other assets. A business owner who sells his firm, for example, will appear wealthy in the year of the sale because of the large capital gain realized at that time, even though the increase in the firm's value probably accrued over a much longer period. Placing that person near the top of the income distribution in the year of the sale and at a much lower rank in other years misstates his or her economic status in all years, overstating it in one and understating it in all others. Yet in the absence of lifetime income data, it is impossible to accurately apportion the capital gains realized in a single year over multiple years. Analysts must choose between counting the gain as income when realized or allotting only part or none of it to current income.

Extensive examination of tax data on the sales of capital assets indicates that apportioning gains across years on the basis of a single year's realizations would lead to significant error.[5] CBO thus counted all capital gains as income when realized.

APPENDIX B: INEQUALITY INDEXES

This Congressional Budget Office (CBO) analysis uses several indexes to measure the distribution of income and taxes. Those indexes are derived from concentration curves, which generally plot the cumulative distribution of income or taxes against the cumulative distribution of the population. This appendix provides information on the calculation and interpretation of those indexes.

The Gini Index

The Gini index is a widely used measure of income inequality. It ranges from zero to one, with increasing values of the index implying greater inequality.[1] The index provides a useful summary metric, characterizing the entire income distribution with a single number. The Gini index can be derived from data on the shares of income accruing to various income groups. (See Box 2 for more discussion about deriving the index.)

One way to put the Gini index in context is to examine a shift in income shares that produced a particular change in the Gini index. For example, in 2007 the system of government transfers and federal taxes increased the share of income accruing to each of the bottom four quintiles of the population (a quintile is one-fifth of a distribution) by 1 or 2 percentage points (relative to their share of market income) while reducing the share accruing to the highest quintile by around 7 percentage points. Much of that reduction came from the top percentile, whose share of income shrank by 4 percentage points. Those shifts in income shares caused a difference of almost 11 percentage points in the Gini index: The Gini index for market income was 0.590, and the Gini index for after-tax income was 0.483.

Another way to put the Gini index in context is to see the impact that hypothetical income shifts would have on that measure. Shifting money from lower-income groups to higher-income groups would cause the index to rise, whereas shifts from higher- to lower-income groups would cause it to fall. Shifts across large ranges of the income distribution would have a bigger effect on the index than shifts across smaller ranges. A shift of 1 percent of market income from the top percentile of the income distribution to the bottom quintile would lower the Gini index by 0.018 (see Table B-1). That shift, of roughly $95 billion (in 2007 dollars), would reduce income in the highest percentile by about 5 percent but would boost income in the bottom quintile by almost 50 percent. Making that same size shift from the top percentile to the middle quintile would reduce the Gini index by 0.010, and shifting it instead to the 95th to 99th percentiles would lessen the index by only 0.001 percentage point. Shifting 1 percent of income from the middle quintile to the lowest quintile would reduce the index by 0.008, while shifting it to the highest quintile would raise the index by 0.009. Shifting that money from the lowest quintile to the middle or highest quintile would boost the index by 0.008 or 0.017, respectively.

A further way of interpreting the Gini index is as a statistical measure of the dispersion of the income distribution, similar to a standard deviation. In particular, the Gini index can be interpreted and calculated as half of the relative mean difference. The relative mean difference, in turn, is equal to the average difference in income between every pair of households in the population, expressed as a percentage of average income. So the Gini index of 0.590 for market income implies that the average income difference across pairs of households was equal to 118 percent (2 times 0.590) of average household market income, or roughly $66,600. In contrast, the index for after-tax income was 0.483, so the average difference between all households was equal to 97 percent of average after-tax income, or about $47,900.

Income Concentration Indexes

Concentration indexes are similar to the Gini index, expressing the concentration of each income source as a single number. A concentration index differs from a Gini index for each source because in calculating the concentration index, households are ranked by total market income rather than by income from that source, as they would be in calculating the Gini index. The concentration index captures two effects: the concentration of income from that source, and the correlation of that income source with income from other sources (and hence with total market income). The latter effect arises because households are sorted by total market income when computing the metric. Thus, for example, the concentration index for labor compensation has increased over time both because compensation has become more unevenly distributed in favor of higher-compensation households and because compensation has become more highly correlated with other unevenly distributed sources of income, such as capital income.

Decomposing the Gini Index by Income Source

To calculate the Gini index G for total income Y, CBO used a standard formula:

$$G(Y) = \frac{2}{N^2 \bar{Y}} \times \sum_{i=1}^{N} \left(i - \frac{N+1}{2} \right) \times Y_i$$

$$(1)$$

where i is the index for each household ranked by total income, Y, from 1 to N.

Other formulas for estimating the Gini index, such as one based on the covariance of income with the cumulative distribution function of income, yield identical estimates.

The Gini index for total income can be decomposed into contributions from each income source.[2] The decomposition used in this analysis is:

$$G(Y) = \sum_{j=1}^{J} \frac{\bar{y}_j}{\bar{Y}} \times \bar{G}(y_j)$$

$$(2)$$

where:

j is the index for each income source, from 1 to J;

y_j is the income from each source;

y is the average amount of income from each source;

Y is the average amount of total income;

y_j/Y is the share of total income accounted for by each income source; and

$G(y_j)$ is the concentration index for each income source (sometimes called the pseudo-Gini).

Changes in the share of total income accounted for by each income source are reported in the main text as shifts among sources of income. The pseudo-Gini differs from the conventional Gini for the income source because individuals are ranked by total income rather than income from that source. Changes in the pseudo-Gini are reported as an increased concentration of the income source. That term will rise if an income source becomes more concentrated higher in the distribution of total income, which occurs if the source becomes more concentrated by itself or if income from that source becomes closely correlated with income from other sources.

G (y_j) can be written as:

$$\overline{G}(y_j) = \frac{2}{N^2 \overline{y}_j} \times \sum_{i=1}^{N} \left(i - \frac{N+1}{2} \right) \times y_{ij}$$

(3)

CBO's decomposition can be mathematically derived from the three-factor decomposition used by some researchers.[3] That decomposition divides the Gini into three components, using the covariance formula for the Gini coefficient:

$$G(Y) = \sum_{j=1}^{J} \frac{cov\left(y_j, F(Y)\right)}{cov\left(y_j, F(Y_j)\right)} \times \frac{2cov\left(y_j, F(y_j)\right)}{\overline{y}_j} \times \frac{\overline{y}_j}{\overline{Y}}$$

(4)

where F is the cumulative distribution function of income.

The first term is called the Gini correlation; it measures how closely the distribution of income from each income source aligns with the distribution of total income. The second term is the pure Gini for each income source, and the third term is a weight for each income source, equal to its share of total income.

CBO's approach essentially combines the first two terms into one factor. Multiplying the first two terms together yields:

$$G(Y) = \sum_{j=1}^{J} \frac{2cov\left(y_j, F(Y)\right)}{\overline{y}_j} \times \frac{\overline{y}_j}{\overline{Y}}$$

(5)

The first term equals the concentration index for each income source when households are ranked by their total income. It differs from the second term of the previous equation in that the numerator is the covariance of income from source j with the cumulative distribution function of total income Y rather than income source $j(yj)$

Tax Progressivity Indexes

Several indexes have been devised to summarize the progressivity of a tax system. Those indexes rely on so-called Lorenz-type concentration curves to summarize the distribution of the tax system in a single number.

One such measure, known as the Reynolds-Smolensky index, is equal to the difference between the Gini index for before-tax income and the Gini index for after-tax income. If the tax system is proportional (each household pays the same share of income in taxes), then the Gini indexes for before- and after-tax income are identical, and the Reynolds-Smolensky index takes on a value of zero. If the tax system is progressive (average tax rates rise with income), then the Gini index for after-tax income is smaller than the Gini index for before-tax income, and the Reynolds-Smolensky index takes on a positive value.

Another measure, the Kakwani index, is computed as the difference between a concentration index for tax payments (with households ordered by their before-tax household income) and the Gini coefficient for beforetax income. If the tax system is proportional, then the tax concentration index exactly equals the Gini index for before-tax income, and the Kakwani index takes on a value of zero. If the tax system is progressive, then the Kakwani index has a positive value; and if the tax system is regressive, then the Kakwani index has a negative value.

Although both of those indexes measure the progressivity of the tax system, they do so in different ways, which can lead to different conclusions about that progressivity.

The Kakwani index directly measures the concentration of tax payments, comparing that with the concentration of income. The index is thus indifferent to the size of the tax system, viewing the progressivity of the tax system on the basis of the shares of taxes paid and the shares of income received by different income groups. By contrast, the Reynolds-Smolensky index only indirectly measures the concentration of payments, by comparing the distribution of after-tax income to before-tax income. That formula measures the re-distributive effect of the tax system, and it is a function of both the con-centration of tax payments and the share of household income claimed by the tax system.[4] Those two measures can yield different conclusions about the change in progressivity induced by a change in the tax code.

APPENDIX C: THE EFFECT OF HEALTH INSURANCE ON THE DISTRIBUTION OF INCOME

Health insurance represents a significant and growing portion of labor compensation and government transfer payments. Employer-sponsored health insurance (ESI) is the largest component of nonwage compensation provided to workers, and the Medicare and Medicaid programs are two of the largest federal transfer programs. Because receiving health insurance allows households to consume more health care without giving up other forms of consumption, the Congressional Budget Office (CBO) included estimated values of that insurance in household income for this study. Many analyses of household income do not include health insurance, however, at least in part because assigning a value to it is difficult.

This appendix shows how including health insurance affected the estimates of income inequality presented in this study and how valuing Medicare, Medicaid, and the Children's Health Insurance Program (CHIP) in a different way would have led to different estimates. Under either approach to valuing those government transfers, including health insurance in income reduces measured income inequality and the measured increase in inequality between 1979 and 2007.

Assigning a Value to Health Insurance

Receiving health insurance enhances the economic wellbeing of recipients, enabling them to obtain health care services at a reduced out-of-pocket cost. But recipients of health insurance might prefer to receive a cash payment equal to the employer's or government's cost of that insurance because then they could choose whether to use all of that cash payment to purchase insurance on their own or to use some or all of the cash payment for other purposes. Therefore, the value of the health insurance to a recipient might be lower than the cost of providing it, particularly for low-income recipients, whose consumption of other goods and services is tightly constrained by their lack of resources.

In the main analysis of this study, CBO counted the full value of health insurance premiums paid by employers as income.[1] However, CBO counted only the so-called fungible value of Medicare, Medicaid, and CHIP as income. That measure, developed by the Census Bureau and used in some of its income definitions, equals the amount of resources freed up for other uses by that insurance, up to the average cost of those services (total cost to the govern-ment divided by the number of program participants). The fungible value of Medicare, Medicaid, and CHIP for a household thus depends not only on the average cost of the benefits provided by those programs but also on the in-come and needs of the household.[2] This appendix also shows results using the average cost of Medicare, Medicaid, and CHIP rather than the fungible value.

Evaluating the Impact on Income Inequality

Two recent papers have directly examined how the treatment of health insurance affects the measurement of income inequality.[3] In one analysis, Gary Burtless and Pavel Svaton used estimates of the value of health insurance from the Current Population Survey (CPS) and the value of health care services consumed from the Medical Expenditure Panel Survey (MEPS) over the 1996–2005 period. Using the CPS-based measures of health insurance, the authors found that the inclusion of that insurance raised average income by about 8 percent in the first half of that period and by more than 10 percent in the latter half of the period. The relative increases in income were larger in the lower part of the income distribution than in the higher part, so the inclusion of health insurance reduced measured income inequality. The authors also found that including health insurance led to a slower measured increase in income inequality over time. Moreover, the authors found similar effects on inequality when they included the MEPS-based measures of health care consumption in income instead of the CPS-based measures of health insurance.

Richard Burkhauser and Kosali Simon undertook a similar analysis, supplementing income from the CPS with insurance imputations from the MEPS. Specifically, the authors used the MEPS data to construct measures of the insurance value of health insurance rather than using the actual heath care services consumed. They found that including employer-sponsored health insurance in income reduced measured income inequality and the measured increase in income inequality over time. They also found that including the government-provided health insurance programs had an even greater effect on reducing both the level and increase in income inequality.

Employer-Sponsored Health Insurance

Consistent with the results presented in those two papers, CBO found that including employer-sponsored health insurance in income slightly lowered measured inequality and the measured increase in inequality between 1979 and 2007.

Employer-sponsored health insurance provides the biggest proportional boost to income in the middle of the distribution, with a smaller boost at both extremes of the distribution. At the bottom of the income distribution, households are unlikely to have ESI, either because they are not working or because they are employed in jobs that do not offer it. At the top of the income distribution, high-income workers are quite likely to receive ESI, but because the average costs of health insurance do not rise proportionally with income, ESI is a relatively small part of their compensation. Therefore, in 2007, households in the lowest income quintile (or fifth of the distribution) received only 2.2 percent of the total value of ESI, whereas those in the middle quintile received 19.5 percent, and households in the highest quintile received 40 percent (see Table C-1). That insurance represented 1.4 percent of income in the lowest quintile, between 6 percent and 7 percent of income in the middle three quintiles, and declining shares of income moving up within the top quintile to only 0.5 percent of income for the top percentile (see Table C-2).

The Gini index for market income (including ESI) was slightly below that of other market income, indicating more equality (see Figure C-1). That small net effect masks distributional shifts, however. Adding ESI to other income increased income in the middle of the distribution by more than at either end of the distribution. The equalizing effect of increasing income in the middle of the distribution more than at the top was slightly larger than the disequalizing effect of increasing income in the middle more than at the bottom, so the net effect was slightly equalizing. The equalizing effect of ESI has increased a bit over time, in large part because the amount spent on em-ployer-sponsored health insurance has grown faster than other market income.

Medicare, Medicaid, and CHIP

Including receipt of Medicare, Medicaid, and CHIP significantly reduces income inequality because the beneficiaries of both programs are disproportionately represented in the lower part of the income distribution. Only families with income below specified levels are eligible for Medicaid, so very little of the program's impact is on the upper reaches of the income distribution. CHIP also has income limits, though they are generally higher than the limits for Medicaid. In 2007, when measuring Medicaid and CHIP benefits by their average cost, about 65 percent of the benefits accrued to the lowest income quintile and about 18 percent accrued to the second quintile (see Table C-1).[4] The fungible value of Medicaid and CHIP is constructed by the Census Bureau to be less than or equal to the average cost of the benefits, and the difference relative to average cost tends to be greatest for households that have the lowest incomes. Consequently, when measuring Medicaid and CHIP benefits by their fungible value, the distribution of benefits is somewhat less skewed, with the lowest two income quintiles each receiving more than 30 percent of the benefits in 2007.

Compared with Medicaid and CHIP benefits, the distribution of Medicare benefits is not as concentrated in the lower part of the income distribution, but it still tilts notably in that direction. Although Medicare is not means-tested, most beneficiaries are elderly, which is a group with below-average income. In 2007, when measuring Medicare benefits by their average cost, the lowest quintile received about 46 percent of those benefits. As with Medicaid and CHIP, using the fungible value rather than the average cost reduces the impact of the program at the lower end of the income scale.

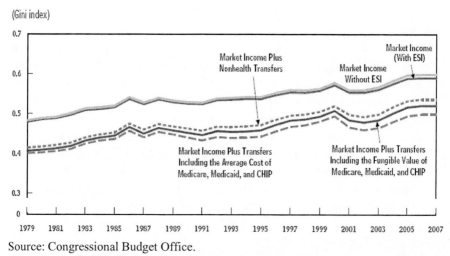

Source: Congressional Budget Office.

Notes: For information on income definitions, the ranking of households, the allocation of taxes, and the construction of inequality indexes, see "Notes and Definitions" at the beginning of this study.

ESI = employer-sponsored health insurance; CHIP = Children's Health Insurance Program.

Figure C-1. Effect of Health Insurance on Income Inequality Measures.

When measuring Medicare benefits by their fungible value, the lowest quintile received about 30 percent of the benefits in 2007.

Table C-1. Shares of Selected Income Measures, by Income Group, 1979 and 2007

	Market Income, Excluding Health Insurance	Employer-Sponsored Health Insurance	Medicare		Medicaid and CHIP		ESI Plus Fungible Value of Medicare, Medicaid, and CHIP
			Average Cost	Fungible Value	Average Cost	Fungible Value	
1979							
Lowest Quintile	7.7	2.9	57.5	47.7	73.5	56.8	19.0
Second Quintile	10.9	13.3	16.6	20.3	14.2	23.9	16.0
Middle Quintile	14.8	20.4	9.0	11.0	5.6	9.1	17.0
Fourth Quintile	21.1	27.3	7.2	8.8	3.7	5.7	20.7
80th–90th Percentiles	14.7	17.1	3.6	4.2	1.2	2.3	12.6
90th–95th Percentiles	9.8	10.0	2.0	2.3	0.6	1.1	7.3
95th–99th Percentiles	11.6	7.5	2.7	3.4	0.6	1.1	5.9
Top 1 Percent	9.6	1.7	1.3	1.7	0	0	1.6
All Quintiles	100.0	100.0	100.0	100.0	100.0	100.0	100.0
2007							
Lowest Quintile	5.7	2.2	46.1	30.1	64.6	31.5	15.5
Second Quintile	8.6	10.1	20.2	25.1	18.1	33.0	17.8
Middle Quintile	12.7	19.5	13.7	18.1	8.7	17.6	18.8
Fourth Quintile	18.6	28.2	9.5	12.7	4.9	10.4	20.7
80th–90th Percentiles	13.6	18.2	4.4	5.8	2.0	3.7	12.2
90th–95th Percentiles	9.8	10.6	2.5	3.4	0.9	1.5	7.0
95th–99th Percentiles	13.0	8.9	2.7	3.6	0.8	1.5	6.2
Top 1 Percent	18.6	2.3	0.9	1.2	0.2	0.5	1.7
All Quintiles	100.0	100.0	100.0	100.0	100.0	100.0	100.0

Source: Congressional Budget Office

Notes: For information on income definitions, the ranking of households, the allocation of taxes, and the construction of inequality indexes, see "Notes and Definitions" at the beginning of this study.

CHIP = Children's Health Insurance Program; ESI = employer-sponsored health insurance.

Table C-2. Health Insurance as a Share of Market Income, by Income Group, 1979 and 2007

	Market Income, Excluding Health Insurance	Employer-Sponsored Health Insurance	Medicare Average Cost	Fungible Value	Medicaid and CHIP Average Cost	Fungible Value	ESI Plus Fungible Value of Medicare, Medicaid, and CHIP
				1979			
Lowest Quintile	1.0	10.7	7.1		4.9	2.1	10.1
Second Quintile	4.1	2.7	2.6		0.8	0.8	7.4
Middle Quintile	4.1	1.0	0.9		0.2	0.2	5.2
Fourth Quintile	3.7	0.5	0.5		0.1	0.1	4.3
80th–90th Percentiles	3.3	0.4	0.3		0	0	3.7
90th–95th Percentiles	2.9	0.3	0.3		0	0	3.2
95th–99th Percentiles	1.8	0.3	0.3		0	0	2.2
Top 1 Percent	0.5	0.2	0.2		0	0	0.7
All Quintiles	3.1	1.6	1.3		0.6	0.3	4.7
				2007			
Lowest Quintile	1.4	29.1	14.1		20.9	3.2	18.6
Second Quintile	6.3	12.5	11.5		5.8	3.3	21.0
Middle Quintile	6.9	4.8	4.7		1.6	1.0	12.6
Fourth Quintile	6.4	2.1	2.1		0.6	0.4	8.8
80th–90th Percentiles	5.4	1.3	1.3		0.3	0.2	6.9
90th–95th Percentiles	4.3	1.0	1.0		0.2	0.1	5.4
95th–99th Percentiles	2.6	0.8	0.8		0.1	0.1	3.5
Top 1 Percent	0.5	0.2	0.2		0	0	0.6
All Quintiles	4.3	4.3	3.2		2.2	0.7	8.1

Source: Congressional Budget Office.

Notes: For information on income definitions, the ranking of households, the allocation of taxes, and the construction of inequality indexes, see "Notes and Definitions" at the beginning of this study.

CHIP = Children's Health Insurance Program; ESI = employer-sponsored health insurance.

From 1979 to 2007, total spending on Medicare, Medicaid, and CHIP grew rapidly, so the increment to households' incomes from the programs grew rapidly as well. When valued at average cost, Medicare benefits rose from 1.6 percent to 4.3 percent of market income over that period, while Medicaid and CHIP benefits rose from 0.6 percent to 2.2 percent. The fungible value of Medicare, Medicaid, and CHIP benefits did not grow nearly as rapidly as the average cost of those programs, but it still grew more rapidly than market income. Between 1979 and 2007, the fungible value of Medicare benefits increased from 1.3 percent to 3.2 percent of market income, and the fungible value of Medicaid and CHIP benefits increased from 0.3 percent to 0.7 percent. The growth of those programs relative to market income increased the redistributive effect of those programs. But the programs became less concentrated in the bottom of the distribution (whether measured by insurance value or fungible value), which partially offset that increase in the redistributive effect.

Including Medicare, Medicaid, and CHIP benefits in income lowers the measured Gini index (see Figure C-1). In 1979, the Gini index for market income plus transfers including the fungible value of Medicare and Medicaid benefits was 0.407, compared with the Gini index for market income plus transfers apart from Medicare, Medicaid, and CHIP of 0.415—a reduction of about 2 percent. Including benefits from those programs at their average cost would further lower the Gini index to 0.401. In 2007, including the fungible value of Medicare, Medicaid, and CHIP benefits reduced the Gini index by 3 percent, from 0.537 to 0.521. Including the average cost instead would have decreased the Gini index further, to 0.499.

End Notes for Summary

1. For information on income definitions, the ranking of households, the allocation of taxes, and the construction of inequality indexes, see "Notes and Definitions" at the beginning of this study. All measures of household income are adjusted to account for differences in household size. Appendix A provides a more detailed discussion of the methodology.
2. This study does not include state and local taxes, an issue discussed in more detail in Appendix A.
3. In this study, CBO measured dispersion using the Gini index, which takes on the value of zero if income is equally distributed and increases as incomes become more unequal.

End Notes

[1]. Arthur F. Jones Jr. and Daniel H. Weinberg, *The Changing Shape of the Nation's Income Distribution, 1974–1998,* Current Population Reports, Series P60-204 (Bureau of the Census, June 2000); and Michael Strudler and others, *Analysis of the Distribution of Income, Taxes, and Payroll Taxes via Cross Section and Panel Data, 1979–2004* (Internal Revenue Service, Statistics of Income Division, 2006).

[2]. Tabulations of tax returns from the Internal Revenue Service show that high-income taxpayers had especially large declines in adjusted gross income between 2007 and 2009. However, evidence based solely on survey data from the Census Bureau shows some increase in income dispersion between 2007 and 2009. (See Internal Revenue Service, *Statistics of Income—Individual Income Tax Returns*, for 2007, 2008 and 2009; and U.S. Census Bureau, Current Population Survey, 1968 to 2010 Annual Social and Economic Supplements, "Selected Measures of Household Income Dispersion: 1967 to 2009," www.census.gov/hhes/www/income/ data/historical/inequality/taba2.pdf.)

[3]. Organization for Economic Cooperation and Development, *Growing Unequal? Income Distribution and Poverty in OECD Countries* (2008).

[4]. Thomas Piketty and Emmanuel Saez, "Income Inequality in the United States, 1913–1998," *Quarterly Journal of Economics*, vol. 118, no. 1 (February 2003), pp. 1–39.

[5]. The recession in 1980 officially began in January 1980, and the most recent recession began in December 2007.

[6]. Households are ranked by income that is adjusted for household size by dividing income by the square root of a household's size. Each fifth of the population (quintile) contains an equal number of people, but because households vary in size, quintiles generally contain unequal numbers of households. (See Appendix A for the income ranges for each quintile.)

[7]. As a point of comparison, by one calculation the Gini index for the United States in the mid-2000s was about 23 percent above the average for all OECD countries and about 23 percent below the index for Mexico, the OECD country with the highest index. See Organization for Economic Cooperation and Development, *Growing Unequal? Income Distribution and Poverty in OECD Countries.*

[8]. See Piketty and Saez, "Income Inequality in the United States," and updated tables at www.econ.berkeley.edu/ ~saez/.

[9]. Carmen DeNavas-Walt, Bernadette D. Proctor, and Jessica C. Smith, *Income, Poverty, and Health Insurance Coverage in the United States: 2009,* Current Population Reports, Series P60-238 (Bureau of the Census, September 2010).

[10]. Richard Burkhauser and others, *Estimating Trends in US Income Inequality Using the Current Population Survey: The Importance of Controlling for Censoring,* Working Paper 14247 (Cambridge, Mass.: National Bureau of Economic Research, August 2008).

[11]. A concentration index differs from a Gini index for each source because in calculating the concentration index, the population is ranked by total market income rather than by income from that source, as they would be in calculating the Gini index for that source. A concentration index can thus range from -1.0 (if all income from a source accrued to the household with the lowest market income), to 0 (if the income from a source was evenly distributed across households), to 1.0 (if all income from a source accrued to the household with the highest market income).

[12]. Congressional Budget Office, *Changes in the Distribution of Workers' Hourly Wages Between 1979 and 2009* (February 2011).

[13]. David H. Autor, Lawrence F. Katz, and Melissa S. Kearney, "Trends in U.S. Wage Inequality: Revising the Revisionists," *Review of Economics and Statistics*, vol. 90, no. 2 (May 2008), pp. 300–323.

[14]. Claudia Goldin and Lawrence F. Katz, "Long-Run Changes in the U.S. Wage Structure: Narrowing, Widening, Polarizing," *Brookings Papers on Economic Activity*, no. 2 (Fall 2007), pp. 135–165.

[15]. David Lee, "Wage Inequality in the United States During the 1980s: Rising Dispersion or Falling Minimum Wage?" *Quarterly Journal of Economics*, vol. 144, no. 3 (August 1999), pp. 977–1023.

[16]. David Card, Thomas Lemieux, and Craig Riddell, "Unions and Wage Inequality," *Journal of Labor Research*, vol. 25, no. 4 (December 2004), pp. 519–562.

[17]. Paul Krugman, "Trade and Wages, Reconsidered," *Brookings Papers on Economic Activity*, no. 1 (Spring 2008), pp. 103–154.

[18]. Congressional Budget Office, *The Role of Immigrants in the U.S. Labor Market* (November 2005); and David Card, *Immigration and Inequality*, Working Paper 14683 (Cambridge, Mass.: National Bureau of Economic Research, January 2009).

[19]. Congressional Budget Office, *Changes in the Distribution of Workers' Annual Earnings Between 1979 and 2007* (October 2009).

[20]. Sheldon Danziger, "Do Working Wives Increase Family Income Inequality?" *Journal of Human Resources*, vol. 15, no. 3 (Summer 1980), pp. 444–451; Lynn A. Karoly and Gary Burtless, "Demographic Change, Rising Earnings Inequality, and the Distribution of Personal Well-Being," *Demography*, vol. 32, no. 3 (August 1995), pp. 379–405; Gary Burtless, *Effects of Growing Wage Disparities and Changing Family Composition on the US Income Distribution*, Working Paper 4 (Center on Social and Economic Dynamics, July 1999); and three articles by Maria Cancian and Deborah Reed: "The Impact of Wives' Earnings on Income Inequality: Issues and Estimates," *Demography*, vol. 36, no. 2 (May 1999), pp. 173–184, and "Sources of Inequality: Measuring the Contributions of Income Sources to Rising Family Income Inequality, *Review of Income and Wealth*, vol. 47, no. 3 (September 2001), pp. 321–333, and "Assessing the Effects of Wives' Earnings on Family Income Inequality," *Review of Economics and Statistics*, vol. 80, no. 1 (February 1998), pp. 95–107.

[21]. CBO has estimated the split of earnings between spouses based on a combination of information reported on tax forms and in the Current Population Survey and examined the effect on household income dispersion of the earnings of so-called secondary earners—the spouses with lower earnings. The Gini index for household income including the earnings of secondary earners was about 1 percent lower than the Gini index excluding those earnings over the 1979–2007 period.

[22]. A recent paper argues that any substantial increase in U.S. income inequality from 1993 to 2004 is confined to the top percentile of the income distribution (see Burkhauser and others, *Estimating Trends in US Income Inequality*). In contrast, CBO finds that the growth in income for the top percentile accounted for just a bit more than half of the rise in market income inequality over that period.

[23]. See Congressional Budget Office, *Capital Gains Taxes and Federal Revenues* (October 2002).

[24]. Piketty and Saez, "Income Inequality in the United States."

[25]. Sherwin Rosen, "The Economics of Superstars," *American Economic Review*, vol. 71, no. 5 (December 1981), pp. 845–858.

[26]. For a review of that literature, see Robert J. Gordon and Ian Dew-Becker, "Selected Issues in the Rise of Income Inequality," *Brookings Papers on Economic Activity,* no. 2 (Fall 2007), pp. 169–190.

[27]. Steven N. Kaplan and Joshua D. Rauh, "Wall Street and Main Street: What Contributes to the Rise in the Highest Incomes?" *Review of Financial Studies,* vol. 23, no. 3 (March 2010), pp. 1004–1050.

[28]. Jon Bakija, Adam Cole, and Bradley T. Heim, *Jobs and Income Growth of Top Earners and the Causes of Changing Income Inequality: Evidence from U.S. Tax Return Data,* Working Paper 2010-24 (Williamstown, Mass: Williams College, November 2010).

[29]. Thomas Philippon and Ariell Reshef, *Wages and Human Capital in the U.S. Financial Industry: 1909–2006,* Working Paper 14644 (Cambridge, Mass.: National Bureau of Economic Research, January 2009).

[30]. This study does not include state and local taxes, an issue discussed in more detail in Appendix A.

[31]. Fungible value is a measure developed by the Census Bureau and used in its alternative income definitions. It is generally the amount of resources freed up for other uses by the services provided through a transfer program; the measure is intended to capture the value of the in-kind benefit to the recipient. The fungible value of Medicare, Medicaid, and the Children's Health Insurance Program has grown more slowly than expenditures for those programs because the fungible value is constrained by slow income growth among low-income recipients. Appendix C provides more details on the concept, as well as a general discussion of the effect of health care benefits on measures of income inequality.

[32]. Transfers as measured in this study do not equal total government expenditures on the same transfer programs, for several reasons. Importantly, health care programs are valued at their fungible value as defined by the Census Bureau, not by their expenditures. Also, some transfer payments are received by individuals not in the scope of the Census Bureau's survey data, such as the institutionalized population, and some recipients misreport the amount of transfer payments they receive.

[33]. Information used in this study on recipients and benefit amounts for Social Security and unemployment insurance came primarily from tax returns.

[34]. In this analysis, the full amount of the earned income tax credit, including the refundable portion, is counted as a reduction in federal taxes (although some of those amounts are paid to people because they exceed the recipients' other tax liabilities).

[35]. An increase in the refundable portions of the earned income tax credit and the child tax credit (which are not counted as transfers here) largely offsets the decline in transfer payments to lowincome families with children.

[36]. CBO's measure of federal taxes includes individual and corporate income taxes, social insurance (payroll) taxes, and excise taxes. CBO did not include state and local taxes in this analysis because of the difficulty of estimating them over a long time period. It is unclear how that omission affects conclusions about the redistributive effect of taxes (see Appendix A for more discussion).

[37]. Although Social Security payroll taxes are not progressive, the program as a whole is generally thought to be progressive because the ratio of the lifetime benefits received from Social Security to the lifetime payroll taxes paid for the program is higher for people with lower lifetime earnings than for people with higher earnings. See Congressional Budget Office, *Is Social Security Progressive?* (December 2006).

[38]. In addition to federal individual income taxes and payroll taxes, total federal taxes include federal taxes on corporate income and federal excise taxes. Those sources accounted for 94

percent of federal receipts in fiscal year 2010. The federal estate tax, customs duties, and miscellaneous receipts are not included in the analysis.

[39]. A related tax progressivity index, the Suits Index, shows similar trends in tax progressivity over time.

End Notes for Appendix A

[1]. See Daniel H. Weinberg, "Income Data Quality Issues in the Annual Social and Economic Supplement to the Current Population Survey" (paper prepared for the American Enterprise Institute–University of Maryland Seminar on Poverty Measurement, October 12, 2004).

[2]. For example, a household consisting of a married couple with two children with income of $80,000 would have an adjusted income of $40,000 ($80,000 divided by $\sqrt{4}$) and would have the equivalent economic ranking of a single person with income of $40,000 or a married couple with income of about $56,600 ($56,600 divided by $\sqrt{2}$ is approximately $40,000). See Constance F. Citro and Robert T. Michael, eds., *Measuring Poverty: A New Approach* (Washington, D.C.: National Academy Press, 1995).

[3]. See Jane G. Gravelle and Kent A. Smetters, "Does the Open Economy Assumption Really Mean That Labor Bears the Burden of a Capital Income Tax?" *Advances in Economic Analysis & Policy*, vol. 6, no. 1, Article 3 (2006); Alan J. Auerbach, "Who Bears the Corporate Tax? A Review of What We Know," in James M. Poterba, ed., *Tax Policy and the Economy*, vol. 20 (Cambridge Mass.: MIT Press, 2006), pp. 1–40; William M. Gentry, *A Review of the Evidence on the Incidence of the Corporate Income Tax,* Office of Tax Analysis Paper 101, Washington, D.C., 2007; William C. Randolph, *International Burdens of the Corporate Income Tax,* Congressional Budget Office Working Paper 2006-09 (August 2006); and Jennifer C. Gravelle, *Corporate Tax Incidence: Review of General Equilibrium Estimates and Analysis,* Congressional Budget Office Working Paper 2010-03 (May 2010).

[4]. For distributional analyses of state and local tax systems, see Joseph A. Pechman, *Who Paid the Taxes: 1966–85?* (Washington, D.C.: Brookings Institution, 1985); and Donald Phares, *Who Pays State and Local Taxes?* (Cambridge, Mass.: Oelgeschlager, Gunn, and Hain, 1980). For more-recent estimates, see Andrew Chamberlain and Gerald Prante, *Who Pays Taxes and Who Receives Government Spending? An Analysis of Federal, State, and Local Tax and Spending Distributions, 1991–2004*, Working Paper 1 (Washington, D.C.: Tax Foundation, March 22, 2007); and Institute on Taxation and Economic Policy, *Who Pays? A Distributional Analysis of the Tax Systems in All 50 States* (November 2009).

[5]. See Congressional Budget Office, *Perspectives on the Ownership of Capital Assets and the Realization of Capital Gains* (May 1997).

End Notes for Appendix B

1. Researchers have developed several other inequality indexes. For a comparison of the properties of different measures, see Frank A. Cowell, *Measuring Inequality* (New York: Oxford University Press, 2011).

2. This derivation is reported in A.F. Shorrocks, "Inequality Decomposition by Factor Components," *Econometrica,* vol. 50, no. 1 (January 1982), pp. 193–211; and John C. H. Fei, Gustav Ranis, and Shirley Kuo, "Growth and the Family Distribution of Income by Factor Components," *Quarterly Journal of Economics*, vol. 92, no.1 (February 1978), pp. 17–53.

3. See Robert I. Lerman and Shlomo Yitzhaki, "Income Inequality Effect by Income Source: A New Approach and Applications to the United States," *Review of Economics and Statistics*, vol. 67 (1985), pp. 151–156.

4. In fact, the indexes can be mathematically derived from each other primarily on the basis of the average tax rate. The Reynolds-Smolensky index is equal to the Kakwani index multiplied by the inverse of the after-tax rate, plus an adjustment for the difference between the before-tax and after-tax income rankings. See John Creedy, "Taxation Redistribution and Progressivity: An Introduction," *Australian Economic Review,* vol. 32, no. 4 (December 1999), pp. 410–422.

End Notes for Appendix C

[1]. The Census Bureau estimates the value of employers' contributions to health insurance on the basis of a separate survey of employers. A full description of the methods used to value noncash benefits is provided in Appendix B of Bureau of the Census, *Measuring the Effect of Benefits and Taxes on Income and Poverty: 1992*, Current Population Reports, Series P60, No. 186RD (September 1993), pp. viii-ix and B-1 to B-5.

[2]. For each household, the Census Bureau compares the household's income to an estimate of the cost to the household of meeting basic needs for food and housing. If a household does not have enough income to meet those basic needs, the Census Bureau assumes that the household would spend nothing on health care in the absence of the government transfer programs, and it sets the fungible value for health care benefits for that household equal to zero. For households with some income above what is necessary to meet basic needs, the fungible value is set equal to the amount of income above that basic standard, up to the average cost of the health care benefits. The Census Bureau estimates the average cost of health care benefits using outlays for Medicare, Medicaid, and CHIP by state and risk class.

[3]. See Gary Burtless and Pavel Svaton, "Health Care, Health Insurance, and the Distribution of American Incomes," *Forum for Health Economics & Policy,* vol. 13, no. 1 (Frontiers in Health Policy Research), Article 1; and Richard V. Burkhauser and Kosali I. Simon, *Measuring the Impact of Health Insurance on Levels and Trends in Inequality,* Working Paper 15811 (Cambridge, Mass.: National Bureau of Economic Research, March 2010).

[4]. The Census Bureau combines its estimates of the value of Medicaid and CHIP benefits, so CBO did not analyze those programs separately.

In: Income Inequality
Eds: R. D. Alford and R. Reilly

ISBN: 978-1-61942-511-8
© 2012 Nova Science Publishers, Inc.

Chapter 2

CHANGES IN THE DISTRIBUTION OF WORKERS' ANNUAL EARNINGS BETWEEN 1979 AND 2007[*]

Congressional Budget Office

NOTES

Many of the figures in this report use shaded vertical bars to indicate periods of recession. (A recession extends from the peak of a business cycle to the trough.)

All earnings, which were adjusted for inflation using the price index for personal consumption expenditures, are reported in 2007 dollars.

Supplemental data for this analysis will be available on CBO's Web site (www.cbo.gov).

PREFACE

This Congressional Budget Office (CBO) paper, which was prepared at the request of the Senate Committee on Finance, documents changes in the annual earnings of workers ages 25 to 54 between 1979 and 2007. CBO's

---

[*] This is an edited, reformatted and augmented version of a Congress of the United States Congressional Budget Office publication, dated October 2009.

analysis compares the distribution of earnings for male and female workers and documents changes in the annual earnings of workers with very high earnings. The analysis also examines changes in earnings mobility (the rate at which workers move from one position in the distribution to another) and earnings variability (the extent to which a worker's earnings change from one year to the next). In keeping with CBO's mandate to provide objective, impartial analysis, this paper makes no recommendations.

Molly Dahl and Jonathan A. Schwabish wrote the paper under the guidance of Joyce Manchester and Bruce Vavrichek. Helpful comments came from Nabeel Alsalam, Patrick Bernhardt, David Brauer, Jeffrey Kling, Ben Page, and Frank Sammartino, all of CBO; from Paul Cullinan and Ralph Smith, formerly of CBO; and from Lawrence Katz of Harvard University and Alan B. Krueger of Princeton University, currently serving as the Department of the Treasury's Assistant Secretary for Economic Policy. (The assistance of external reviewers implies no responsibility for the final product, which rests solely with CBO.)

Leah Mazade edited the report, and Christine Bogusz proofread it. Maureen Costantino designed the cover and prepared the paper for publication, with assistance from Holly Battelle, Priscila Hammett, and Christian Howlett. Lenny Skutnik produced the initial copies, Linda Schimmel coordinated the print distribution, and Simone Thomas prepared the electronic version for CBO's Web site.

Douglas W. Elmendorf
Director
October 2009

INTRODUCTION AND SUMMARY

Understanding how the annual earnings of workers have changed over time is integral to projecting possible changes in such earnings in the future and considering government tax and spending policies that affect workers. This Congressional Budget Office (CBO) paper documents changes in workers' annual earnings; however, it does not delve deeply into the causes of those changes or the possible implications for government policy.

The paper first describes changes between 1979 and 2007 in the annual (inflation-adjusted) earnings of workers ages 25 to 54. CBO found that men with relatively low, median, and relatively high earnings (specifically, men at the 10th, 50th, and 90th percentiles of their earnings distribution) earned more than women in the same position of their own earnings distribution in 2007, and that those differences were smaller in 2007 than in 1979 (see Figure 1). (Box 1 presents a primer on some of the measurement concepts used in this paper.) CBO also compared the differences in earnings between low, median, and high earners of the same sex in a given year. For men, the ratio of the earnings of high earners to those of median earners was larger in 2007 than in 1979, whereas the earnings ratio for median and low earners was roughly the same in the two years. For women, in contrast, the ratio of the earnings of high earners to those of median earners was roughly the same in 2007 as it was in 1979, but the earnings ratio for median and low earners was smaller in 2007 than it was in 1979.

This paper also documents changes between 1989 and 2005 in the annual (inflation-adjusted) earnings of workers ages 25 to 54 with very high earnings. (Examining workers with earnings at the very top of the distribution requires a different data set, one that does not span all of the years covered by the data set used in the first part of the paper.) CBO found that men with earnings at the top of their earnings distribution (those at the 95th and 99th percentiles) earned more than women at the top of their distribution in each year, although that difference declined over time. The earnings of men and women at the top of their earnings distributions were higher in 2005 than they were in 1989, and the increase for workers at the 99th percentile of the distribution was larger than for workers at the 95th percentile. Also, the share of earnings held by workers in the top 5 percent of the distribution increased between 1989 and 2005.

Additionally, CBO examined changes in earnings mobility and variability. Dividing the population into five groups based on earnings, CBO found that the fraction of people moving from one group to another (for example, from the bottom fifth of the distribution to the top fifth) over various five-year spans was roughly unchanged from 1989 to 2005 for both men and women. Slightly more than one-quarter of men and of women experienced increases or decreases in earnings of 50 percent or more between 2004 and 2005. The percentage was similar for year-over-year changes throughout the 1989–2005 period.

There are several points to keep in mind in considering CBO's findings. First, this paper examines annual earnings, not hourly wages. People's annual earnings are determined both by their earnings per hour and by how many hours they work each year. Second, people's annual earnings are not necessarily the entirety of their compensation. In focusing on earnings for its analysis, CBO did not take into account other forms of compensation, such as defined-benefit retirement plans, employers' contributions to 401(k) plans, or employment-based health insurance. (Comprehensive data on compensation for individuals are not generally available over long periods.) Third, annual earnings do not necessarily represent all of the resources available to workers. Many people receive income from unemployment compensation, child support, or other sources over the course of a year. Also, many people share resources with family members, and some people have savings on which they can rely. Fourth, CBO excluded people who had no earnings over the course of a year and those who had earnings only from self-employment. People who had both earnings and income from self-employment were included in the analysis, but their income from self-employment was not considered. Finally, CBO's restriction of the analysis to people ages 25 to 54 lessened the effects that individuals' decisions about educational attainment and retirement might have on the study's results.

Box 1. A Primer on Measuring Earnings Dispersion, Mobility, and Variability

This report examines men and women at selected percentiles of their respective earnings distribution. To make that idea more concrete, consider 200 workers—100 men and 100 women—ages 25 to 54 on an auditorium stage. The men line up separately from the women; each group arranges itself, from left to right, by people's earnings. Thus, the worker with the lowest earnings stands closest to the left wall of the stage, and the worker with the highest earnings stands closest to the right wall. Each line, or array, of workers represents the entirety of the earnings distribution of men or women ages 25 to 54 in a given year.

The 10th worker from the left in either line has relatively low earnings. That man or woman is at the 10th percentile of his or her respective earnings distribution, which means that 10 percent of the workers of the same sex have the same or lower earnings and 90 percent have higher earnings. The worker standing in the very middle of each line has earnings in the middle, or at the median, of his or her earnings distribution. That worker is at the 50th percentile of the distribution (50 percent of workers of the same sex have the same or lower earnings and 50 percent have higher earnings), and so on.

In its analysis, the Congressional Budget Office (CBO) found that in 2007, men tended to earn more than women.

Consider the 200 men and women standing in two lines on the stage in the auditorium. They stand shoulder to shoulder, and the line of women is in front of the line of men. The 10th man from the left (who is at the 10th percentile of the earnings distribution of men) had higher earnings than the woman standing directly in front of him (who is at the 10th percentile of the earnings distribution of women). The same is true of the men and women at the 50th and the 90th percentiles.

CBO's analysis also considered changes in the dispersion of earnings. In 2007, the earnings of the man at the 90th percentile of his earnings distribution were about 7 times those of the man at the 10th percentile, and the earnings of the woman at the 90th percentile of her earnings distribution were 8.5 times those of the woman at the 10th percentile. Consider the people standing on the stage again, but now they have spread out across the stage in such a way that the man earning $10,000 is twice as far from the wall on the left as the man earning $5,000. The women have spread out in the same way. The man at the 90th percentile is seven times farther from the wall on the left than the man at the 10th percentile; the woman at the 90th percentile is 8.5 times farther than the woman at the 10th percentile.

The results of CBO's analysis that have been discussed here thus far are based on a "snapshot" of the workforce in 2007. To follow the same people over time, CBO used a different data set. That information allowed analysts to document two longitudinal concepts of changes in earnings: earnings mobility and earnings variability.

The example of the auditorium stage remains useful. Now, all of the seats in the audience are full of people of all ages. In 2000, all the working men and women who are 25 to 54 years of age are invited to come up on stage and form two lines—the men in one and the women in the other, ordered as before (from left to right) by the amount of their earnings. Each person is given a placard that has "2000" written on it as well as a number indicating whether they are in the lowest 20 percent of the distribution, between the 21st and 40th percentiles, and so on. (That assignment divides the earnings distributions into fifths, or quintiles.) In 2005, all of the same people return to the auditorium—audience members as well as people who were on the stage—and all the working men and women ages 25 to 54 are again invited to come up onto the stage. Some of the people on stage will have placards from 2000; some will not. In particular, people who were younger than 25 in 2000 or were not working then will not have placards.

Some of the people remaining in the audience will have placards from

2000 as well; those people are now either beyond the 25-to-54 age range of people invited up on stage or were working in 2000 but are not working in 2005.

The men and women on the stage again form separate lines, by increasing order of their earnings in 2005, and each is given a placard that has "2005" and their position in the distribution on it. All of the people that have placards from both 2000 and 2005 step forward and are asked to examine the changes in their quintiles between the two years. The results illustrate the idea of earnings mobility, or how people move around in the earnings distribution relative to each other.

Keeping the men and women separate, CBO found that about half of the men and half of the women in its sample were in the same segment of the earnings distribution in 2005 as they had been in 2000.

The second longitudinal concept of changes in earnings, that of earnings variability, does not directly relate to the auditorium full of workers.

Earnings variability, as CBO defined it for this analysis, captures the fraction of workers that experienced a large change in their earnings from one year to the next. About 27 percent of men and 29 percent of women experienced increases or decreases in earnings of 50 percent or more between 2004 and 2005.

TRENDS IN EARNINGS BETWEEN THE 10TH AND 90TH PERCENTILES OF THE EARNINGS DISTRIBUTION

For this part of its analysis, CBO examined trends in the annual earnings of workers ages 25 to 54 between 1979 and 2007, focusing on workers at the 10th, 50th, and 90th percentiles of the earnings distribution. The data CBO used were drawn from the Census Bureau's Current Population Survey (CPS), which contains information on the characteristics of workers and the number of hours they work.[1] (The appendix discusses the CPS, including the limitations that it presented for CBO's analysis.) Both 1979 and 2007 represent a trough in the unemployment rate of people ages 25 to 54, which makes results from those years roughly comparable. More recent data, for 2008, are also available (see Box 2).

CBO's analysis centered on individuals with wage and salary earnings; it excluded people who had no earnings as well as those who had earnings only from self-employment. All earnings, which were adjusted for inflation using the price index for personal consumption expenditures, are reported in 2007 dollars.

Comparing Trends in the Earnings of Men and Women between 1979 and 2007

As a point of reference, in 2007, workers at the 10th percentile of the combined earnings distribution of men and women earned $10,800; those at the median, or 50th percentile, earned $35,000; and those at the 90th percentile earned $85,000 (see Table 1).

Men and Women at the Median

In contrast to the annual earnings of men at the median of their earnings distribution—which, in inflation-adjusted terms, were the same in 2007 as for their counterparts in 1979—the annual earnings of women at the median of their distribution were 60 percent higher in 2007 than for their counterparts in 1979 (see Table 1 and Figure 2).

Box 2. Earnings of Men and Women in 2008

Using the most recent data available, the Congressional Budget Office found that the real (inflation-adjusted) annual earnings of men and women at the 10th, 50th, and 90th percentiles of their earnings distributions declined between 2007 and 2008. In 2007, the unemployment rate for people ages 25 to 54 was 3.7 percent, a trough in the unemployment rate for that age group; in 2008, the rate was 4.8 percent.

All indications are that the unemployment rate for that group will be higher still in 2009.

The annual earnings of men at the 10th percentile of their earnings distribution were 14 percent lower in 2008 than they were for their counterparts at the 10th percentile in 2007. That change represents the largest year-to-year decline in earnings for that group between 1979 and 2008. Men at the median of the earnings distribution earned $39,700 in 2008, 3 percent less than their counterparts earned in the previous year. The earnings of men at the 90th percentile in 2008 were $96,800, also 3 percent lower than their counterparts' earnings in 2007.

The annual earnings of women at the 10th, 50th, and 90th percentiles of their earnings distribution also declined between 2007 and 2008.

The earnings of women at the 10th percentile were $7,700 in 2008, 4 percent lower than those of women at the same point in the distribution in 2007. The annual earnings of women at the median and the 90th per centile declined by 3 percent and 2 percent, respectively, between 2007 and 2008.

Real Annual Earnings of Workers at Selected Percentiles of the Earnings Distribution, by Sex (2007 dollars)

	2007	2008	Percentage Change
		All Workers	
10th Percentile	10,800	9,700	-10
50th Percentile	35,000	33,900	-3
90th Percentile	85,000	83,200	-2
		Men	
10th Percentile	14,600	12,600	-14
50th Percentile	41,000	39,700	-3
90th Percentile	100,000	96,800	-3
		Women	
10th Percentile	8,000	7,700	-4
50th Percentile	30,000	29,000	-3
90th Percentile	68,000	66,800	-2

Source: Congressional Budget Office based on the Census Bureau's March Current Population Surveys.

Note: The sample that CBO used consisted of people ages 25 to 54 with earnings, which included wages and salaries but excluded income from self-employment. Earnings were adjusted for inflation using the price index for personal consumption expenditures and rounded to the nearest $100.

The earnings of men at the median of their earnings distribution followed the ups and downs of the business cycle: That is, they fell during recessions and in the years surrounding such downturns, and they rose during expansions—periods of stronger economic growth (see Figure 2). During the recessions in the early 1980s, the inflation-adjusted earnings of men at the median of their earnings distribution dropped, and although those earnings increased over the next several years, the upswings were offset by subsequent declines between 1988 and 1992, a period that included another recession. The earnings of men at the median of the distribution increased again between 1994 and 2000 (a period of relatively strong economic growth); they remained relatively unchanged between 2001 and 2007.

In contrast to the pattern seen for men, the inflation-adjusted earnings of women at the median of their earnings distribution rose at a relatively steady pace between 1979 and 2000 (see Figure 2). That increase was driven in part by substantial increases in the number of hours women worked. In 1979, 67 percent of women who had earnings near the median of their earnings distribution worked full-time for the entire year; in 2000, 81 percent of women who had earnings near the median were full-time, full-year workers (see Table 2). (For this analysis, CBO defined full-time, full-year employment as usually working 35 or more hours per week and working at least 50 weeks of the year.) Between 2000 and 2007, the rise in the earnings of women at the median of their distribution slowed.

Men and Women at the 10th Percentile

The annual earnings of men at the 10th percentile of their earnings distribution in 2007 were $14,600, an amount slightly smaller than the inflation-adjusted earnings of their 1979 counterparts (see Table 1). In contrast, the annual earnings of women at the 10th percentile of their distribution in 2007 were $8,000, more than three times the earnings of their 1979 counterparts.

The earnings of men at the 10th percentile between 1979 and 2007 tended to be more responsive to changes in economic conditions than the earnings of men at the 50th percentile. Nevertheless, the cumulative change in earnings between 1979 and 2007 for both groups was quite similar (see Figure 2 on).

The tripling of earnings for women at the 10th percentile of their distribution over the 1979–2007 period was spurred by substantial increases in the number of hours that women in that group worked. In 1979, 4 percent of women at the 10th percentile of their earnings distribution were working full-time all year long; by 2007, that figure had risen to 18 percent (see Table 2).

Men and Women at the 90th Percentile

The earnings of men and women at the 90th percentile of their respective earnings distributions were higher in 2007 than they were for their counterparts in 1979. Men at the 90th percentile of their distribution in 2007 earned $100,000— 33 percent more than the inflation-adjusted earnings of their 1979 counterparts. Women at the 90th percentile of their distribution in 2007 earned $68,000, or 71 percent more than their 1979 counterparts earned.

Much of the cumulative increase in earnings between 1979 and 2007 for men at the 90th percentile can be attributed to a rise in their earnings during the late 1990s (see Figure 2). In contrast, the cumulative increase in earnings for women at that percentile over the same period resulted from more consistent year-over-year changes in earnings.

Comparing Men's and Women's Earnings in 2007

The annual earnings of men at the 10th, 50th, and 90th percentiles of their earnings distribution in 2007 were $14,600, $41,000, and $100,000, respectively. The annual earnings of women at the same relative positions of their own earnings distribution were $8,000, $30,000, and $68,000 (see Table 1). That is, the earnings of men were 1.8, 1.4, and 1.5 times those of their counterpart women.

Men's annual earnings over the 1979–2007 period tended to be higher than women's in part because men tended to work more hours over the course of a year than women did (see Table 2). Not only were men more likely to be employed full-time for the entire year, but among workers who reported full-time, full-year employment, the average number of hours worked was generally somewhat greater among men than among women.[2] That finding also held true among people who reported part-time or part-year employment: Men generally worked more hours over the course of a year than did women.

The differences between men and women in the number of hours worked over the course of a year do not fully account for the differences between their annual earnings. Even among those who worked a similar number of hours, men tended to earn more than women. To put it another way, the hourly wage of men tended to be higher than that of women. The differences between men's and women's hourly wages may be due to differences in education, experience in the labor force, the occupation or industry in which people worked, preferences or tastes (say, for relatively dangerous work, which may pay more, all else being equal), discrimination, or other factors. A thorough analysis of factors that contribute to differences in earnings is outside the scope of this paper.[3]

Changes in the Dispersion of Men's and Women's Earnings between the 10th and the 90th Percentiles of Their Earnings Distributions

In 2007, the earnings of men at the 90th percentile of the distribution were about seven times those of men at the 10th percentile (see the ratios in Table 1). That relationship represented an increase in dispersion over that existing in 1979, when the earnings of men at the 90th percentile of the distribution were five times those of men at the 10th percentile.

A widening in the upper portion of the distribution of men's earnings was the major contributor to the widening of earnings between the 90th and 10th percentiles. Dispersion in the lower portion of the distribution of men's earnings in 1979 was slightly less than it was in 2007— that is, the earnings of men at the 50th percentile of their earnings distribution were 2.7 times those of men at the 10th percentile in 1979, compared with 2.8 times in 2007 (see Table 1). In contrast, the earnings of men at the 90th percentile of their distribution in 1979 were 1.8 times those of men at the 50th percentile; by 2007, that gap had widened to 2.4 times.

Comparing dispersion in the bottom half of the men's earnings distribution in 2007 with that prevailing in 1979 masks some of the underlying changes in dispersion over time. For instance, from 1979 to 1982 and again from 1989 to 1992, the earnings of men at the 10th percentile of the distribution declined by more than did the earnings of those at the 50th percentile (see Figure 2); the larger drop led to a widening of the dispersion in the bottom half of the distribution during those times (see Figure 3). Conversely, between 1993 and 1998—a period of relatively strong economic growth—the earnings of men at the 10th percentile of the distribution increased by more than did those of men at the 50th, leading to a narrowing of the dispersion in the bottom half of the distribution during that time.[4]

Among women, a steady narrowing occurred between 1979 and 2007 in the dispersion of earnings between the 10th and 90th percentiles of their earnings distribution (see Table 1). In 1979, women at the 90th percentile of the distribution earned 15.3 times more than women at the 10th percentile; by 2007, that ratio was 8.5 times.

The narrowing that occurred for women between the 10th and the 90th percentiles was driven by the substantial increase in earnings (208 percent) at the 10th percentile and the subsequent decline in dispersion in the bottom half of the distribution (see Figure 2 and Figure 3). In comparison, the changes in earnings for women at the median and for women at the 90th percentile of their earnings distribution were similar between 1979 and 2007 (see Figure 2). Relatively little change in dispersion was seen in the top half of the women's distribution (see Figure 3).

TRENDS IN EARNINGS AT THE TOP
OF THE EARNINGS DISTRIBUTION

As another part of its analysis, CBO examined trends in the annual earnings of workers ages 25 to 54 between 1989 and 2005, specifically focusing on workers at the 90th percentile or higher of the earnings distribution. For those calculations, CBO used data from the Continuous Work History Sample (CWHS) provided by the Social Security Administration, a data set that contains limited demographic information about the members of the sample beyond their age and sex. However, the data set does contain detailed information about the earnings of the very highest earners. (In contrast, the CPS—the data set used for the analysis in the previous section— does not.) The most recent year of data from the CWHS available to CBO at the time of the analysis was 2005. Although that year does not represent a trough in the unemployment rate of people ages 25 to 54 (as 1989 does), the unemployment rate in 2005 was 4.1 percent, which is comparable to the unemployment rate of 4.2 percent for that age group in 1989. (The appendix discusses both data sets, including the limitations each presented for CBO's analysis.)

Comparing Trends in the Earnings of Men and Women at the Top of Their Distributions between 1989 and 2005

As a point of reference, workers at the 95th percentile of the combined earnings distribution of men and women in 2005 earned $103,200 (in 2007 dollars); those at the 99th percentile earned $214,600 (see Table 3).

Men and Women at the 95th Percentile
Men at the 95th percentile of their earnings distribution in 2005 earned $123,400, an increase of 24 percent over their counterparts' inflation-adjusted earnings in 1989. Women at the 95th percentile of their earnings distribution earned $79,400 in 2005—37 percent more than their counterparts earned in 1989 (see Table 3).

The real annual earnings of women at the 95th percentile of their earnings distribution increased in every year between 1989 and 2005 (see Figure 4). In contrast, the earnings of their counterpart men increased during the period of strong economic growth in the late 1990s but declined during the recessionary periods of the early 1990s and early 2000s.

Men and Women at the 99th Percentile
Men at the 99th percentile of their earnings distribution in 2005 earned $278,100, and women at the 99th percentile of their distribution in that year earned $139,100. Those amounts were 30 percent and 60 percent more, respec-

tively, than the inflation-adjusted earnings of their counterparts in 1989 (see Table 3).

The real annual earnings of women at the 99th percentile increased in almost every year between 1989 and 2005. One exception was between 2000 and 2002, around the time of the 2001 recession, when earnings for those women were relatively unchanged. In contrast, during that recession, the earnings of their counterpart men declined significantly (see Figure 4).

Comparing Men's and Women's Earnings at the Top of Their Distributions in 2005

Among the highest earners, men earned more than women. In 2005, the earnings of men at the 95th and 99th percentiles of their distribution were 1.6 and 2.0 times those of women in the same relative positions in their distribution. In comparison, in 1989, the earnings of men at the 95th and 99th percentiles were 1.7 and 2.5 times those of women in the same relative positions. Those differences in men's and women's earnings in 2005 were smaller than the differences in 1989 (see Table 3).

Changes in the Dispersion of Men's and Women's Earnings at the Top of Their Distributions

In 2005, the earnings of men at the 99th percentile of their earnings distribution were 3.0 times those of men at the 90th percentile. That ratio represented an increase in dispersion compared with that in 1989, when the ratio was 2.8 times. In 2005, the earnings of women at the 99th percentile of their earnings distribution were 2.2 times those of women at the 90th percentile, representing an increase in dispersion, compared with the ratio in 1989 of 1.8 times (see Table 3).

The patterns of changes in dispersion for men between the 99th and 90th percentiles of their earnings distribution and between the 99th and 95th percentiles were similar over the years 1989 to 2005. In both cases, dispersion tended to increase during periods of relatively strong economic growth and to decline during periods of relatively weak economic growth (see Figure 5)

Like the patterns of changes in dispersion that CBO found in men's earnings, the patterns between the 99th and 90th percentiles and between the 99th and 95th percentiles of the women's earnings distribution were similar:

Over the 1989–2005 period, dispersion was more likely to decline during times of relatively weak economic growth (for instance, during and immediately following the 2001 recession) and to increase during times of relatively strong economic growth (for instance, during the mid- to late 1990s) (see Figure 5).

CHANGES IN SHARES OF EARNINGS

The increase in earnings that CBO found at the top of the distribution was associated with an increase in the share of earnings received by those in the top 5 percent of the distribution.

The share of earnings going to men in the top 5 percent of the distribution—that is, to men whose earnings placed them at or above the 95th percentile of their earnings distribution—was larger in 2005 than in 1989. The top 5 percent of working men ages 25 to 54 received 22 percent of the earnings going to all men in that age range in 1989 and 26 percent of earnings going to all men in that age range in 2005.[5] In that year, the top 1 percent of working men—those with earnings of $278,100 or more—garnered 13 percent of all earnings, up from 10 percent in 1989 (see Figure 6).

The share of earnings that men with the highest earnings received followed the ups and downs of the business cycle to some extent between 1989 and 2005. The largest increases in the share of earnings going to the top 5 percent of workers occurred from the mid- to late 1990s, a period of relatively strong economic growth. During the periods of weaker economic growth that surrounded the recessions in 1990 to 1991 and in 2001, the share of earnings accruing to the top 5 percent of men remained unchanged or contracted.[6]

The share of earnings received by the top 5 percent of women, like that of their counterpart men, also rose between 1989 and 2005, although the share of earnings received by the top 5 percent of women was smaller than it was for men. The top 5 percent of women ages 25 to 54 with earnings received 17 percent of the earnings going to all women in that age range in 1989 and 20 percent of such earnings in 2005.[7] Those shares are about 5 to 7 percentage points lower than the share of earnings received by men in the top 5 percent of their earnings distribution. In 2005, the top 1 percent of women ages 25 to 54 with earnings received about 8 percent of the earn ings going to all women in that age group, up from about 5 percent in 1989 (see Figure 6).

The share of earnings that the highest-earning women received was less sensitive to the business cycle between 1989 and 2005 than the corresponding share for men. During the period of rapid economic growth during the mid- to late 1990s, the share of earnings received by men in the top 5 percent of their distribution grew more quickly than the share of earnings received by women in the top 5 percent of their distribution. As the economy slowed during the 2001 recession, the share of earnings going to men in the top 5 percent of their earnings distribution fell more quickly than did the share of earnings going to women in the top 5 percent.

EARNINGS MOBILITY AND EARNINGS VARIABILITY

Comparing the earnings of people at selected points in the earnings distribution in one year with the earnings of their counterparts in another year does not capture whether a particular individual experiences gains or losses in his or her earnings over time. For example, CBO's finding that the earnings of men at the median of their distribution were, in inflation-adjusted terms, about the same in 2007 as they were in 1979 does not mean that men with median earnings in 1979 did not experience any gains or losses in earnings in the following years. To measure different aspects of changes in individuals' earnings from one year to another, CBO examined two distinct longitudinal concepts:

- *Earnings mobility,* which measures the probability that workers will change their position in the earnings distribution from one year to another (for example, the probability that a worker will move from the bottom part of the earnings distribution in one year to the top part of it in another); and
- *Earnings variability,* which measures the percentage change in a person's earnings from one year to the next.

Earnings mobility is a relative concept: Whether an individual changes position in the earnings distribution depends not only on the changes in his or her own earnings but on the changes in everyone else's earnings as well.

In contrast, earnings variability is not relative. How one person's earnings change from one year to the next is not directly related to changes in other people's earnings.

Earnings Mobility

One method of measuring earnings mobility is to split the earnings distribution for one year into five equally sized pieces, or quintiles; group the lowest 20 percent of earners together, and so on, up the distribution; do the same for a later year; and determine what percentage of people switched groups.

Earnings Mobility between 2000 and 2005

Table 4 and Table 5 show the probability of a person's moving from one quintile in 2000 to another quintile in 2005 as well as the probability of moving into or out of the very top of the distribution. For example, of the men who were in the middle quintile (the 41st to the 60th percentile) of their earnings distribution in 2000 and were working in 2005, 8 percent were in the lowest quintile, 42 percent were in the middle quintile, and 6 percent were in the highest quintile in 2005.[8]

About half of the men and half of the women in the bottom quintile of their respective earnings distributions in 2000 were in the bottom quintile again in 2005 (see Tables 4 and 5). The pace of mobility from the bottom of the distribution was approximately the same for both men and women: 28 percent of men and 30 percent of women moved up exactly one quintile, and an additional 22 percent of men (12 + 7 + 3) and 25 percent of women (14 + 7 + 4) moved up two or more quintiles between 2000 and 2005.

Workers were more likely to move up the distribution than to move down. Thirty percent of men and 30 percent of women were in a higher quintile of the distribution in 2005 than in 2000. Smaller percentages—17 percent of men and 19 percent of women—were in lower quintiles in 2005 than in 2000.

Workers who were in the top part of the distribution in 2000 tended to be there again in 2005. Eighty percent of men and 77 percent of women in the highest quintile in 2000 were also in the highest quintile in 2005. At the very top of the distribution, about 60 percent of the men and approximately the same percentage of the women who were in the top 1 percent of their respective distributions in 2000 were in the top 1 percent in 2005.

Earnings Mobility by Age

CBO found less mobility across quintiles of the earnings distribution between 2000 and 2005 among older workers—whose careers and earnings may be more stable—than among their younger counterparts (see Figure 7). In other words, the probability of moving from one quintile of the earnings distribution in 2000 to another in 2005 declined with age. Among the youngest workers in the sample (those ages 25 to 29 in 2000 and 30 to 34 in 2005), almost 60 percent changed quintiles between 2000 and 2005. For the oldest workers in the sample (those ages 50 to 54 in 2005), roughly 40 percent changed quintiles between the two years.

Trends in Earnings Mobility between 1990 and 2005

Mobility across quintiles of the earnings distribution was largely unchanged between 1990 and 2005 (see Figure 8).[9] Among people ages 25 to 54 who were working in both 1990 and 1995, 47 percent were in a different quintile of the earnings distribution in 1995 than they were in 1990—the same rate of mobility found among people working in 2000 and 2005. Most workers who changed quintiles between 1990 and 1995 were moving up the earnings distribution.

CBO examined several different ways of constructing transition tables to analyze earnings mobility (see Box 3). Those methods produced results that were for the most part similar to the findings presented in this part of the analysis.

Earnings Variability

To examine the variability in workers' earnings, CBO calculated the percentage change in earnings from one year to the next for each worker and then grouped those changes into four separate categories: declines and increases greater than 50 percent and declines and increases between 25 percent and 50 percent.[10]

Box 3. Alternative Methods for Analyzing Earnings Mobility

In addition to its main conclusions regarding earnings mobility, the Congressional Budget Office (CBO) also examined mobility using three broad types of alternative techniques.

First, CBO examined how the earnings mobility results presented in Table 4 and Table 5 would change if those transition tables were defined in such a way that the percentage of people moving up the distribution had to equal the percentage of people moving down the distribution. For CBO's main analysis, a person's position in the earnings distribution in a given year was determined by comparing that person's earnings with the earnings of all other workers ages 25 to 54 in that year. That determination

---

was made for workers in that age range in 2000 and again for workers in that range in 2005.

Transitions were defined only for people who were in the sample in both years. Consider a man age 53 in 2000 who was at the 75th percentile of the earnings distribution. In 2005, that same man was 58 years old and outside the age range that CBO examined in this study. As such, his place in the earnings distribution in 2005 was not determined, and no transition was defined for him. Transitions were not defined for workers who were age 50 or older in 2000, who were age 29 or younger in 2005, or who worked in one year but not the other. As a result, the percentage of people who moved up by at least one quintile did not have to equal the percentage of people who moved down by at least one quintile.

Restricting the earnings distribution in each year to include only those workers who were in the sample in both years (that is, who were ages 25 to 54 and working in both 2000 and 2005) results in slightly different outcomes. Under that method, for every person who moves up the distribution, one person must move down. The percentage of men who changed quintiles between 2000 and 2005 was about 1 percentage point lower than the main results presented in this report. The percentage of men who moved up at least one quintile was 6 percentage points lower, and the percentage who moved down at least one quintile was 5 percentage points higher. The differences for women were similar. That is, the percentage of women who changed quintiles between 2000 and 2005 was slightly lower than in the paper's main findings. That slight decline was the result of a drop in the percentage of women who moved up at least one quintile and an increase in the percentage of women who moved down at least one quintile.

Second, CBO examined how the trends in earnings mobility over time differed if the effects of changes in the age distribution of workers over time were removed. Consider a scenario in which there are a relatively large number of young workers. Younger workers tend to have higher rates of mobility than older workers have, so as that large group of young workers aged, mobility might decline. That decline might not represent an actual shift in the mobility of workers but rather the aging of younger workers and the associated decline in mobility. To investigate how the aging of the population might affect the trends in earnings mobility presented in this paper, CBO first fixed the age distribution of the sample population at its 2005 levels. As a second alternative, it adjusted the percentage change in earnings for each worker from one year to another using the median percentage change in earnings among the worker's age group.

Neither adjustment had much of an impact on the trends in estimated rates of mobility.

Third, CBO examined earnings mobility by using a three-year average (rather than a single year) of earnings. Using three years of earnings rather than one dampens the effects that temporary changes in a person's earnings (either unusually high or unusually low earnings in a single year) might have on estimated rates of mobility. That approach resulted in a slightly lower rate of overall mobility for men and virtually no change in the rate of overall mobility for women. For men, nearly all of the change in mobility between the one-year and the three-year-average approach came from a decline in the percentage of workers who moved up the earnings distribution. The percentage of men who moved down the distribution did not change substantially. For women, there was a slight decline in the percentage of workers who moved up the distribution, which was offset by a slight increase in the percentage of workers who moved down the distribution. The trends in mobility over time were similar to the main findings presented in the analysis.

Between 1990 (the first year for which CBO calculated a change over the preceding year) and 2005, the frequency of large—greater than 50 percent—changes in earnings tended to move in concert with economic conditions for both men and women (see Figure 9). That is, during periods of relatively weak economic growth—in particular, during the recessions of 1990 to 1991 and 2001—the fraction of men and women that experienced large year-over-year gains in earnings tended to decline, and the fraction that experienced large year-over-year losses in earnings tended to increase.[11]

The fraction of men and women that experienced more modest changes in earnings—between 25 percent and 50 percent over the previous year—did not fluctuate much between 1990 and 2005. Approximately 7 percent of workers experienced such increases in earnings, and about 4 percent to 5 percent of workers experienced such declines.

EXPLAINING PATTERNS IN EARNINGS AND IN DISPERSION

The distribution of earnings in a particular year is a function of who works, how many hours they work, and the wage they earn per hour. Those three factors interact in a complex fashion. Whether or not an individual chooses to work depends in part on what that person is paid or believes he or she will be paid (the expected wage rate) and the value of the person's time outside of work. The number of hours people work during the year also depends on their hourly wage. If a person's hourly wage increases, he or she may prefer to work more, as each hour spent not working becomes more costly (in terms of forgone earnings). Or the person may prefer to work less—to earn the same amount of money as before but by working fewer hours. In addition, a person's hourly wage depends not only on that individual's characteristics but also on the characteristics of all other workers and potential workers (the supply of labor) and the demand for those characteristics in the labor market.

Who Worked? The Composition of the U.S. Workforce

Between 1979 and 2007, the composition of the U.S. workforce changed. Women constituted a larger share of the workforce in 2007 than they did in 1979. Also, the share of workers that were foreign born was larger in 2007 than in 1994, the first year for which data on immigration were available in the Current Population Survey. Moreover, workers in 2007 had, on average, more education than workers had in 1979. Increased rates of disability and incarceration also played a role in changing the composition of the workforce.

Women as a Share of the Workforce
Between 1979 and 2007, the percentage of women who participated in the paid workforce increased markedly. Although approximately 85 percent of men ages 25 to 54 worked in each year between 1979 and 2007, the fraction of women in that age range who worked grew throughout the 1980s and 1990s, from 66 percent in 1979 to 76 percent in 2000. Between 2000 and 2007, the fraction of women working declined somewhat, falling to 74 percent in 2007 (see Figure 10). As a result of the growing percentage of women who worked, women made up a larger share of the workforce in 2007 than they did in 1979 (see Table 6).

Foreign-Born People as a Share of the Workforce
In 1994, about 11 percent of workers ages 25 to 54 were immigrants; in 2007, that percentage was nearly 17 percent (see Table 6). The growth in the fraction of workers that were immigrants was similar among men and women. In 1994, about 12 percent of working men were immigrants; in 2007, that fraction was about 19 percent. Among women, about 9 percent of working

women in 1994 were immigrants; in 2007, about 15 percent were immigrants.[12]

Workers' Educational Attainment

The educational attainment of working men and women rose between 1979 and 2007, although the increase in attainment for women was greater than that for men (see Table 7). In 1979, a smaller percentage of working women than men (41 percent compared with 48 percent) reported some education beyond high school. Between 1979 and 2000 those percentages increased for both groups. However, between 2000 and 2007, the percentage of working men who reported some education beyond high school did not increase much at all, whereas the percentage of working women who reported such studies continued to increase. In 2007, a larger percentage of working women (67 percent) than of working men (58 percent) reported some education beyond high school.

Disability. For some people, income from disability benefits provides a viable alternative to low-paying jobs.[13] Between 1979 and 2007, the number of people who received disability benefits in a given year increased by roughly two and a half times. Nearly all of that increase occurred after 1990.[14]

Incarceration. Between 1979 and 2007, the rate of incarceration for men—that is, the number of male state or federal prisoners under state or federal jurisdiction as a percentage of all men who were U.S. residents—increased from 0.26 percent to nearly 1.0 percent.[15] Younger men—most, presumably, with skills and job qualifications that are well below average—account for most of the increase in the prison population and are, as a consequence, no longer able to participate in the workforce.[16]

How Much Did Workers Work?

Men and women in the workforce in 2007 worked more over the course of the year than did their counterparts in 1979. The percentage of working men who were employed full-time for at least 50 weeks of the year increased from 78 percent in 1979 to 84 percent in 2007 (see Figure 11). That increase in the percentage of men working on a full-time, full-year basis was not the result of consistent year-over-year increases. Rather, the percentage of working men who worked full-time for at least 50 weeks of the year fell during periods of relatively weak economic growth and rose during periods of relatively strong growth. Among working women, the percentage employed on a full-time, full-year basis climbed from 51 percent in 1979 to 70 percent in 2007. Unlike the increase for men, that rise was the result of relatively consistent year-over-year increases.

How Much Were Workers Paid per Hour?

For men, changes in the average hourly wage (adjusted for inflation) varied across the earnings distribution. The hourly wages of men near the 10th percentile of the earnings distribution were lower in 2007 than the hourly wages of their counterparts in 1979. In contrast, the hourly wages of men near the 90th percentile of the earnings distribution were higher in 2007 than those of their counterparts in 1979 (see Table 8).

For women, hourly wages generally increased between 1979 and 2007. The rise in hourly wages over that period was larger for women near the 90th percentile of their earnings distribution than for women near the 50th percentile. It was also larger for women near the 50th percentile than for women near the 10th percentile (see Table 8).[17]

The Importance of Hours Worked Versus Wages Earned

Because of the complex interplay between the number of hours people work and the hourly wage they earn, it is difficult to precisely break down the changes in earnings over time into the portion attributable to changes in hours and the portion attributable to changes in wages. As a result, most studies that CBO reviewed that attempt to explain changes in distributions over time focus on hourly wages alone. A thorough treatment of that literature is beyond the scope of this paper, although it is an avenue of research that CBO is pursuing.

The rise in earnings between 1979 and 2007 for women at the 10th percentile of their earnings distribution was due in large part to increases in the number of hours those women worked. CBO found that women at the 10th percentile of the earnings distribution in 1979 worked about 550 hours per year; their counterparts in 2007 worked more than twice as many hours, or about 1,210 hours per year.

The decline in earnings between 1979 and 2007 for men at the 10th percentile of their earnings distribution occurred in spite of an increase in the number of hours they worked. In 1979, men at the 10th percentile of the earnings distribution worked 1,700 hours per year; in 2007, they worked 1,790 hours per year, for an increase of about 5 percent. That boost in hours, coupled with the decline in the annual earnings of men at the 10th percentile, implies that those men experienced a decline in their real hourly wages.

Most men and women with relatively high earnings were working a relatively large number of hours in 1979. The increase in earnings between 1979 and 2007 is mostly attributable to increases in the real hourly wage they were paid rather than to further increases in the number of hours they worked.

Table 1. Real Annual Earnings of Workers at Selected Percentiles of the Earnings Distribution, by Sex

	1979	1989	2000	2007		Percentage Change		
					1979–1989	1989–2000	2000–2007	1979–2007
					All Workers			
Earnings (2007 dollars) 10th percentile	5,800	6,900	10,600	10,800	19	54	2	86
50th percentile	29,500	30,600	35,300	35,000	4	15	-1	19
90th percentile	62,500	68,800	82,400	85,000	10	20	3	36
Ratios 50th to 10th percentile	5.1	4.4	3.3	3.2	-14	-25	-3	-37
90th to 50th percentile	2.1	2.2	2.3	2.4	5	5	4	14
90th to 10th percentile	10.9	10.0	7.8	7.9	-8	-22	1	-28
					Men			
Earnings (2007 dollars) 10th percentile	15,000	12,200	15,300	14,600	-19	25	-5	-3
50th percentile	41,000	38,200	42,400	41,000	-7	11	-3	0
90th percentile	75,000	79,500	96,300	100,000	6	21	4	33
Ratios 50th to 10th percentile	2.7	3.1	2.8	2.8	15	-10	0	4
90th to 50th percentile	1.8	2.1	2.3	2.4	17	10	4	33
90th to 10th percentile	5.0	6.5	6.3	6.9	30	-3	10	38
					Women			
Earnings (2007 dollars) 10th percentile	2,600	4,400	7,100	8,000	69	61	13	208
50th percentile	18,800	22,900	28,200	30,000	22	23	6	60
90th percentile	39,700	49,700	61,500	68,000	25	24	11	71
Ratios 50th to 10th percentile	7.2	5.3	4.0	3.8	-26	-25	-5	-47
90th to 50th percentile	2.1	2.2	2.2	2.3	5	0	5	10
90th to 10th percentile	15.3	11.4	8.7	8.5	-25	-24	-2	-44

Source: Congressional Budget Office based on the Census Bureau's March Current Population Surveys.

Note: The sample that CBO used consisted of people ages 25 to 54 with earnings, which included wages and salaries but excluded income from self-employment. Earnings were adjusted for inflation using the price index for personal consumption expenditures and rounded to the nearest $100.

Table 2. Employment Characteristics of Workers at Selected Percentiles of the Earnings Distribution, by Sex

	1979	1989	2000	2007
		Men		
		Percentage of Workers Employed Full-Time and for the Full Year		
10th Percentile	40	43	65	60
50th Percentile	87	90	93	92
90th Percentile	94	96	96	96
		Average Hours Worked per Year by Full-Time, Full-Year Workers		
10th Percentile	2,270	2,250	2,180	2,170
50th Percentile	2,260	2,290	2,310	2,290
90th Percentile	2,380	2,410	2,460	2,450
		Average Hours Worked per Year by Part-Time or Part-Year Workers		
10th Percentile	1,320	1,310	1,380	1,230
50th Percentile	1,620	1,750	1,640	1,670
90th Percentile	1,580	1,910	1,710	1,710
		Women		
	Percentage of Workers Employed Full-Time and for the Full Year			
10th Percentile	4	6	15	18
50th Percentile	67	76	81	83
90th Percentile	87	89	87	90
	Average Hours Worked per Year by Full-Time, Full-Year Workers			
10th Percentile	2,410	2,290	2,100	2,120
50th Percentile	2,080	2,120	2,140	2,140
90th Percentile	2,160	2,230	2,280	2,250
	Average Hours Worked per Year by Part-Time or Part-Year Workers			
10th Percentile	480	720	890	1,000
50th Percentile	1,480	1,460	1,380	1,430
90th Percentile	1,650	1,630	1,650	1,540

Source: Congressional Budget Office based on the Census Bureau's March Current Population Surveys.

Note: The sample that CBO used consisted of people ages 25 to 54 with earnings, which included wages and salaries but excluded income from self-employment. CBO defined full-time, full-year workers as those who usually work 35 or more hours per week and work 50 or more weeks per year and part-time or part-year workers as those who usually work less than 35 hours per week or work fewer than 50 weeks per year. Estimates for workers at the 10th percentile of the distribution are averages for workers whose earnings put them between the 8th and 12th percentiles of the distribution. Estimates for workers at the 50th and 90th percentiles were similarly calculated.

Table 3. Real Annual Earnings of Workers at Selected Percentiles at the Top of the Earnings Distribution, by Sex

	1989	2000	2005		Percentage Change	
				1989–2000	2000–2005	1989–2005
				All Workers		
Earnings (2007 dollars)90th percentile[a]	65,100	75,200	78,000	16	4	20
95th percentile	82,200	100,100	103,200	22	3	26
99th percentile	159,800	216,700	214,600	36	-1	34
Ratios 95th to 90th percentile	1.3	1.3	1.3	0	0	0
99th to 95th percentile	1.9	2.2	2.1	16	-5	11
99th to 90th percentile	2.5	2.9	2.8	16	-3	12
				Men		
Earnings (2007 dollars) 90th percentile[a]	76,900	89,900	91,500	17	2	19
95th percentile	99,400	122,400	123,400	23	1	24
99th percentile	213,700	285,700	278,100	34	-3	30
Ratios 95th to 90th percentile	1.3	1.4	1.3	8	-7	0
99th to 95th percentile	2.2	2.3	2.3	5	0	5
99th to 90th percentile	2.8	3.2	3.0	14	-6	7
				Women		
Earnings (2007 dollars) 90th percentile[a]	48,000	57,900	62,200	21	7	30
95th percentile	57,900	73,300	79,400	27	8	37
99th percentile	86,800	130,400	139,100	50	7	60
Ratios 95th to 90th percentile	1.2	1.3	1.3	8	0	8
99th to 95th percentile	1.5	1.8	1.8	20	0	20
99th to 90th percentile	1.8	2.3	2.2	28	-4	22

Source: Congressional Budget Office based on the Social Security Administration's Continuous Work History Sample.

Note: The sample that CBO used consisted of people ages 25 to 54 with earnings, which included wages and salaries, tips, and other forms of compensation but excluded self-employment income and deferred compensation. Earnings were adjusted for inflation using the price index for personal consumption expenditures and rounded to the nearest $100.

[a] Earnings for people at the 90th percentile in the Continuous Work History Sample differ from those in the Census Bureau's Current Population Survey (shown in Table 1). See the appendix for a discussion of the differences between the two data sets.

Table 4. Earnings Mobility of Men, 2000 to 2005

Earnings Category in 2000	Quintile[a]					90th to 94th Percentile	Percentile 95th to 98th Percentile	99th Percen-tile and Above
	Lowest	Second	Middle	Fourth	Highest			
Quintile[a]								
Lowest	50	28	12	7	3	1	0	0
Second	18	41	28	9	3	1	0	0
Middle	8	15	42	29	6	1	1	0
Fourth	5	5	13	51	26	4	1	0
Highest	3	2	3	12	80	24	22	6
90th to 94th Percentile	2	2	3	7	86	39	27	2
95th to 98th Percentile	2	2	2	3	91	16	55	13
99th Percentile and Above	2	1	1	2	93	5	27	58

Source: Congressional Budget Office based on the Social Security Administration's Continuous Work History Sample.

Notes: The sample that CBO used consisted of people ages 25 to 54 with earnings, which included wages and salaries, tips, and other forms of compensation but excluded self-employment income and deferred compensation. Earnings were adjusted for inflation using the price index for personal consumption expenditures. To examine mobility, CBO arrayed workers ages 25 to 54 by their earnings in 2000 and separated them into five equally sized segments (or quintiles). It did the same for workers ages 25 to 54 in 2005. Workers who "changed quintiles" were in a different quintile in 2005 than in 2000. Overall, 47 percent of the men in the sample in 2000 were in a different quintile of the earnings distribution in 2005: 30 percent had moved up at least one quintile, and 17 percent had moved down at least one quintile.

a. The lowest quintile refers to workers whose earnings are at or below the 20th percentile of the distribution, the second quintile to workers with earnings between the 21st and 40th percentiles, and so on.

Table 5. Earnings Mobility of Women, 2000 to 2005

Earnings Category in 2000	Earnings Category in 2005							
	Quintile[a]					90th to 94th Percentile	95th to 98th Percentile	99th Percentile and Above
Quintile[a]	Lowest	Second	Middle	Fourth	Highest			
Lowest	46	30	14	7	4	1	0	0
Second	20	40	26	10	4	1	0	0
Middle	9	16	42	26	6	1	1	0
Fourth	5	6	14	49	25	4	2	0
Highest	3	3	4	13	77	22	21	6
90th to 94th Percentile	3	2	3	7	84	38	24	2
95th to 98th Percentile	3	2	2	4	88	16	54	11
99th Percentile and Above	3	2	2	3	91	5	24	58

Source: Congressional Budget Office based on the Social Security Administration's Continuous Work History Sample.

Notes: The sample that CBO used consisted of people ages 25 to 54 with earnings, which included wages and salaries, tips, and other forms of compensation but excluded self-employment income and deferred compensation. Earnings were adjusted for inflation using the price index for personal consumption expenditures. To examine mobility, CBO arrayed workers ages 25 to 54 by their earnings in 2000 and separated them into five equally sized segments (or quintiles). It did the same for workers ages 25 to 54 in 2005. Workers who "changed quintiles" were in a different quintile in 2005 than in 2000. Overall, 49 percent of the women in the sample in 2000 were in a different quintile of the earnings distribution in 2005: 30 percent had moved up at least one quintile, and 19 percent had moved down at least one quintile.

a. The lowest quintile refers to workers whose earnings are at or below the 20th percentile of the distribution, the second quintile to workers between the 21st and 40th percentiles, and so on.

Table 6. Women and Foreign-Born People as Shares of the Workforce

	1979	1989	1994	2000	2007
Women	44.4.	46.6	47.2	47.8	47.2
Foreign-Born People	n.a	n.a	10.5	13.9	16.9

Source: Congressional Budget Office based on the Census Bureau's March Current Population Surveys.

Notes: The sample that CBO used consisted of people ages 25 to 54 with earnings, which included wages and salaries but excluded income from self-employment.

n.a. = not applicable; data on immigration were not collected before 1994.

Table 7. Demographic Characteristics of Workers, by Sex

	1979	1989	2000	2007
Educational Attainment (Percent)		*Men*		
Less than high school	19.7	13.5	10.4	11.0
High school	32.7	34.8	31.5	30.7
Greater than high school	47.6	51.6	58.1	58.2
Age	37.4	37.3	39.1	39.4
Educational Attainment (Percent)		*Women*		
Less than high school	16.9	10.2	8.2	6.7
High school	42.3	38.8	30.2	26.1
Greater than high school	40.8	51.0	61.6	67.2
Age	37.2	37.4	39.4	39.7

Source: Congressional Budget Office based on the Census Bureau's March Current Population Surveys.

Note: The sample that CBO used consisted of people ages 25 to 54 with earnings, which included wages and salaries but excluded income from self-employment.

Table 8. Real Hourly Wages of Workers at Selected Percentiles of the Earnings Distribution, by Sex

(2007 dollars)	1979	1989	2000	2007
		Men		
10th Percentile	10.20	8.80	9.80	9.70
50th Percentile	19.50	17.90	19.30	19.60
90th Percentile	32.20	34.30	42.80	42.40
		Women		
10th Percentile	8.80	8.10	10.50	10.80
50th Percentile	10.50	12.50	15.40	15.60
90th Percentile	19.70	24.40	29.50	32.50

Source: Congressional Budget Office based on the Census Bureau's March Current Population Surveys.

Note: The sample that CBO used consisted of people ages 25 to 54 with earnings, which included wages and salaries but excluded income from self-employment. Estimates for workers at the 10th percentile of the distribution are averages for workers between the 8th and 12th percentiles of the distribution. Estimates for workers at the 50th and 90th percentiles were similarly calculated. Hourly wages were calculated as annual earnings divided by the multiple of the number of weeks worked during the year and the number of hours usually worked per week. Hourly wages were adjusted for inflation using the price index for personal consumption expenditures.

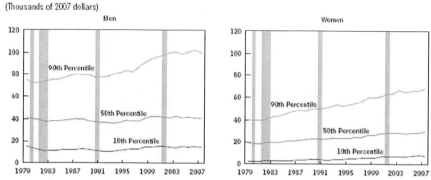

Source: Congressional Budget Office based on the Census Bureau's March Current
    Population Surveys and information on the timing of recessions from the National
    Bureau of Economic Research.

Note: The sample that CBO used consisted of people ages 25 to 54 with earnings,
    which included wages and salaries but excluded income from self-employment.
    Earnings were adjusted for inflation using the price index for personal
    consumption expenditures

Figure 1. Real Annual Earnings of Men and Women at Selected Percentiles of Their
Earnings Distributions.

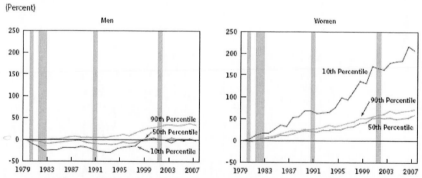

Source: Congressional Budget Office using data on earnings from the Census Bureau's
    March Current Population Surveys and information on the timing of recessions
    from the National Bureau of Economic Research.

Note: The sample that CBO used consisted of people ages 25 to 54 with earnings,
    which included wages and salaries but excluded income from self-employment.
    Earnings were adjusted for inflation using the price index for personal
    consumption expenditures

Figure 2. Cumulative Change in Real Annual Earnings of Men and Women at Selected
Percentiles of Their Earnings Distributions.

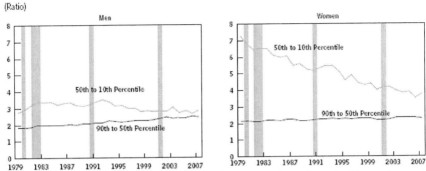

Source: Congressional Budget Office using data on earnings from the Census Bureau's March Current Population Surveys and information on the timing of recessions from the National Bureau of Economic Research.

Note: The sample that CBO used consisted of people ages 25 to 54 with earnings, which included wages and salaries but excluded income from self-employment. Earnings were adjusted for inflation using the price index for personal consumption expenditures

Figure 3.Selected Ratios of Real Annual Earnings of Men and Women at Various Percentiles of Their Earnings Distributions.

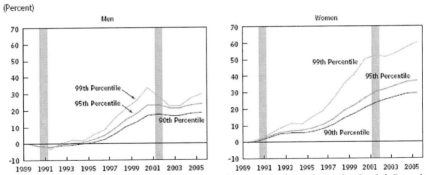

Source: Congressional Budget Office using data on earnings from the Social Security Administration's Continuous Work History Sample and information on the timing of recessions from the National Bureau of Economic Research.

Note: The sample that CBO used consisted of people ages 25 to 54 with earnings, which included wages and salaries, tips, and other forms of compensation but excluded self-employment income and deferred compensation. Earnings were adjusted for inflation using the price index for personal consumption expenditures.

Figure 4. Cumulative Change in Real Annual Earnings of Men and Women at Selected Percentiles at the Top of Their Earnings.

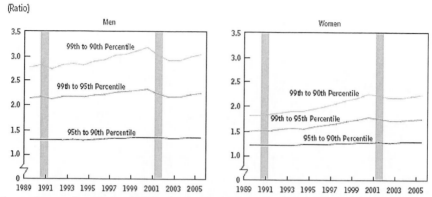

Source: Congressional Budget Office using data on earnings from the Social Security Administration's
Continuous Work History Sample and information on the timing of recessions from the National
Bureau of Economic Research.

Note: The sample that CBO used consisted of people ages 25 to 54 with earnings, which included
wages and salaries, tips, and other forms of compensation but excluded self-employment income
and deferred compensation. Earnings were adjusted for inflation using the price index for
personal consumption expenditures.

Figure 5. Selected Ratios of Real Annual Earnings of Men and Women at Various
Percentiles at the Top of Their Earnings Distributions.

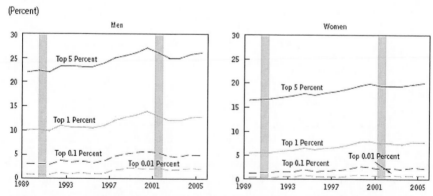

Source: Congressional Budget Office using data on earnings from the Social Security Administration's
Continuous Work History Sample and information on the timing of recessions from the National
Bureau of Economic Research.

Note: The sample that CBO used consisted of people ages 25 to 54 with earnings, which included
wages and salaries, tips, and other forms of compensation but excluded self-employment income
and deferred compensation. Earnings were adjusted for inflation using the price index for
personal consumption expenditures

Figure 6. Shares of Earnings Received by Men and Women in the Top 5 Percent of
Their Earnings Distributions.

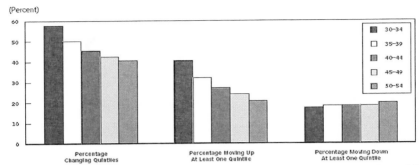

Source: Congressional Budget Office based on the Social Security Administration's Continuous Work History Sample.

Notes: The sample that CBO used consisted of people ages 25 to 54 with earnings, which included wages and salaries, tips, and other forms of compensation but excluded self-employment income and deferred compensation. Earnings were adjusted for inflation using the price index for personal consumption expenditures. To examine mobility, CBO arrayed workers ages 25 to 54 by their earnings in 2000 and separated them into five equally sized segments (or quintiles). It did the same for workers ages 25 to 54 in 2005. Workers who "changed quintiles" were in a different quintile in 2005 than in 2000.

Figure 7. Earnings Mobility of Men and Women Between 2000 and 2005, by Workers' Ages in 2005.

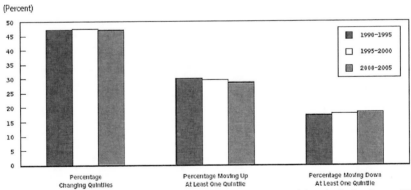

Source: Congressional Budget Office based on the Social Security Administration's Continuous Work History Sample.

Notes: The sample that CBO used consisted of people ages 25 to 54 with earnings, which included wages and salaries, tips, and other forms of compensation but excluded self-employment income and deferred compensation. Earnings were adjusted for inflation using the price index for personal consumption expenditures. To examine mobility, CBO arrayed workers ages 25 to 54 by their earnings in the first year of a period and separated them into five equally sized segments (or quintiles). It did the same for workers ages 25 to 54 five years later. Workers who "changed quintiles" were in a different quintile in the later year than in the earlier year.

Figure 8. Earnings Mobility of Men and Women During Selected Periods.

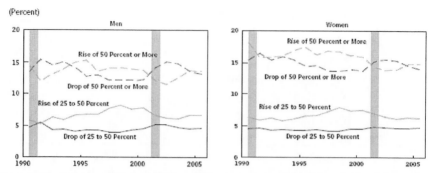

Source: Congressional Budget Office using data on earnings from the Social Security
    Administration's Continuous Work History Sample and information on the timing
    of recessions from the National Bureau of Economic Research.

Note: The sample that CBO used consisted of people ages 25 to 54 with earnings,
    which included wages and salaries, tips, and other forms of compensation but
    excluded self-employment income and deferred compensation. Earnings were
    adjusted for inflation using the price index for personal consumption expenditures.
    The percentage change in earnings is defined here as $((e_t - e_{t-1})/((e_t + e_{t-1})/2)*100)$.

Figure 9. Variability in Men's and Women's Real Annual Earnings.

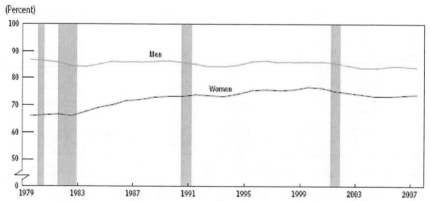

Source: Congressional Budget Office using data on earnings from the Census Bureau's
    March Current Population Surveys and information on the timing of recessions
    from the National Bureau of Economic Research.

Note: The sample that CBO used consisted of people ages 25 to 54 with earnings,
    which included wages and salaries but excluded income from self-employment.

Figure 10. Percentage of People with Positive Annual Earnings, by Sex.

(Percent)

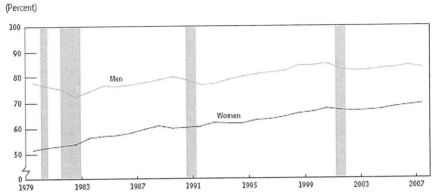

Source: Congressional Budget Office using data on earnings from the Census Bureau's March Current Population Surveys and information on the timing of recessions from the National Bureau of Economic Research.

Note: The sample that CBO used consisted of people ages 25 to 54 with earnings, which included wages and salaries but excluded income from self-employment. Full-time, full-year workers are defined here as those who usually work 35 or more hours per week and work 50 or more weeks per year.

Figure 11. Percentage of Workers Employed Full-Time and for the Full Year, by Sex.

APPENDIX: DATA AND METHODS

To examine earnings between the 10th and 90th percentiles of the earnings distribution, the Congressional Budget Office (CBO) used data from a survey conducted by the Census Bureau, what is now called the Annual Social and Economic Supplement to the Current Population Survey (also known as the March CPS). To examine earnings at the top of the distribution as well as earnings mobility and variability, CBO used data from the Continuous Work History Sample (CWHS) provided by the Social Security Administration (SSA).

CBO's analysis focused on workers ages 25 to 54 during the 1979–2007 period.[1] By restricting the sample to people in that age range, CBO reduced the effect of decisions about education (earlier in life) or retirement (later in life) on its results.

The most recent year for which data were available from the CPS at the time CBO's main analysis was undertaken was 2007; that year also coincided with a "trough" in the unemployment rate—a relatively low 3.7 percent—for people ages 25 to 54. In order to compare similar points in the employment cycle, CBO chose 1979, another trough year, as the initial year of the analysis. In that year, the unemployment rate for that age group was a relatively low 4.2 percent. The two other trough years that fell within the 1979–2007 period were 1989 and 2000, with unemployment rates of 4.2 percent and 3.1 percent, respectively. The part of CBO's analysis that used data from the CWHS begins in 1989, to coincide with that trough year, and ends in 2005, the most recent year of data available to CBO. In 2005, the unemployment rate of people ages 25 to 54 was 4.1 percent, a rate comparable to that in 1989.

All earnings were indexed to 2007 dollars using the price index for personal consumption expenditures (PCE). Another commonly cited measure of consumer price inflation—the research series of the consumer price index for all urban consumers (CPI-U-RS)—tends to grow slightly faster than the PCE price index. In other words, the CPI-U-RS overstates inflation relative to the PCE price index. That is because the CPI-U-RS does not fully account for the extent to which households maintain a standard of living by substituting one product for another when the price of the first product changes relative to the price of all other products. The PCE price index incorporates adjustments that people make over time in the types of goods and services they buy; in contrast, the CPI-U-RS uses a "basket" of products that is assembled according to patterns of consumption that may be as much as two years old.

To examine earnings variability, CBO constructed a measure showing the percentage change in earnings from one year to the next for each individual. That percentage change (known as the arc percentage change) in earnings e is defined here for time period t as $((e_t - e_{t-1})/((e_t + e_{t-1})/2)*100)$. Defining the percentage change in that way allowed CBO to include individuals who move from zero to positive earnings and those who move from positive to zero earnings symmetrically; that is, for example, a person entering employment has a change in earnings of 200 percent, and a person leaving employment has a change of -200 percent. A more traditional definition of percentage change—$((e_t - e_{t-1})/(e_{t-1})*100)$—yields undefined results for workers moving from zero to some earnings (that is, workers for whom e_{t-1} equals zero). Relative to the traditional measure of the percentage change, the arc percentage change used in this analysis understates increases and overstates decreases in earnings.

THE MARCH CURRENT POPULATION SURVEY

The March CPS contains rich demographic and economic information on a large number of households. The data for the main analysis, which were taken from the March CPS for the years 1980 to 2008, refer to calendar years 1979 to 2007. CBO used person-level sample weights that are available in the CPS. That is, the results were weighted in such a way that the sample was nationally representative. The measure of earnings that CBO used in its analysis—annual wages and salaries—does not include income from self-employment.

BENEFITS AND LIMITATIONS OF THE MARCH CURRENT POPULATION SURVEY

A primary benefit of the CPS is that it includes information on the workers it covers (such as their education, the number of weeks they worked, and the number of hours they usually work per week) that goes beyond their earnings. However, survey data are also subject to certain limitations. For instance, some people contacted for the survey will opt not to respond. Others may have difficulty in recalling information, and some may report rounded rather than exact earnings. If a respondent cannot remember or refuses to give his or her earnings, that response may be imputed, or "filled in," by the Census Bureau. Over time, increased rates of imputation and proxy responses (where another person in the household answers for the respondent) might bias the survey's results.[2] And between the 1980 and 2008 surveys, the CPS itself underwent changes in the methods used to collect data, and those changes may affect comparisons over time. For instance, before 1994, the survey was administered on paper; now, the Census Bureau uses computerized survey instruments.[3]

Finally, earnings in the CPS are "top-coded." That means that the files provided for public use do not report earnings above a certain threshold in order to protect the confidentiality of the respondents. The top-coding in the CPS data was the primary reason that CBO used the CWHS to examine the earnings of workers in the top 10 percent of the distribution.

THE CONTINUOUS WORK HISTORY SAMPLE

To examine earnings at the top of the distribution and to document earnings mobility and variability, CBO used data from the CWHS provided by the Social Security Administration. CBO also uses the CWHS for its baseline projections of revenues and outlays related to the Social Security and Medicare programs. An understanding of the trends in the distribution of earnings is an important component of such projections because the programs' revenues and outlays are directly tied to individual workers' earnings through payroll tax and benefit formulas.

The CWHS data set contains longitudinal administrative earnings records for a 1 percent random sample of Social Security numbers. Each year of data between 1989 and 2005 covers more than 800,000 people ages 25 to 54 who have earnings, and recent years contain about 1 million such people. Thus, in the CWHS data set, the top 1 percent of the distribution (above the 99th percentile) includes at least 8,000 workers for any given year. Person-years in which a worker had more than $100 million in earnings (a very small number of observations) were dropped from the sample.

Earnings, as defined in this part of CBO's analysis, include wage and salary earnings, tips, and some other forms of compensation. They exclude self-employment income and deferred compensation, such as contributions to 401(k) accounts.

BENEFITS AND LIMITATIONS OF ADMINISTRATIVE EARNINGS DATA

Using administrative data in an analysis has both benefits and limitations. Among the benefits is that the data used here are not subject to top-coding; that is, information on the very highest earners is retained. Administrative records also provide a consistent measure of earnings for individuals over many years. In addition, the samples are quite large. Furthermore, administrative data are based on employers' reports of individual earnings and therefore are not subject to survey respondents' errors in recall or to issues of rounding or nonresponse.

Although data on earnings in administrative records are generally presumed to be of higher quality than self-reports of earnings in surveys, administrative data do not reflect all types of earnings.[4] Because administrative records are based on earnings as reported by employers for a random sample of Social Security numbers, they miss cash-based employment (or earnings received in the so-called underground economy) as well as the earnings of workers who do not have or do not report a valid Social Security number. The underground economy can include a variety of illegal activities (such as theft) and may also include legal activities by illegal immigrants or compensation paid "under the table." Mark Ledbetter estimates that total wages and salaries paid in the underground economy amount to about 2 percent of the nation's total earnings.[5] Whether the amount of or variability in those earnings has changed significantly over time is unclear. Earnings in the underground economy, which are not reflected in administrative data, may not be captured well in survey data either.

The CWHS data used here capture earnings only from workers in the covered sector—that is, workers who are actively contributing to Social Security. In 1990, 95 percent of paid civilian workers were in the covered sector; in 2002, that share was 96 percent. The majority of uncovered earnings come from state, local, or federal government workers.[6] Including that relatively small sector in the analysis is not likely to have a significant effect on its results.

Another limitation of the administrative data is that they contain almost no information on demographic or household characteristics. Some demographic information, such as year of birth and sex, is available; no information is available on family or household linkages, nonlabor income, or assets.

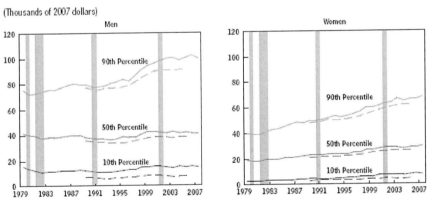

Source: Congressional Budget Office using data on earnings from the Census Bureau's March Current Population Surveys and the Social Security Administration's Continuous Work History Sample, together with information on the timing of recessions from the National Bureau of Economic Research

Notes: Data from the Current Population Survey (CPS) are shown above as solid lines, and data from the Continuous Work History Sample (CWHS) are shown as dashed lines. The sample that CBO used consisted of people ages 25 to 54 with earnings. Earnings from the CPS included wages and salaries but excluded income from self-employment. Earnings from the CWHS included wages and salaries, tips, and other forms of compensation but excluded self-employment income and deferred compensation. Earnings were adjusted for inflation using the price index for personal consumption expenditures.

Figure A-1. Comparing the Real Annual Earnings of Men and Women at Selected Percentiles of Their Earnings Distributions Using Data from the CPS and the CWHS.

COMPARING THE MARCH CURRENT POPULATION SURVEY AND THE CONTINUOUS WORK HISTORY SAMPLE

Between 1989 and 2005, the earnings recorded in the CWHS for men and women ages 25 to 54 at the 10th, 50th, and 90th percentiles of their earnings distributions were generally lower than those reported in the CPS, but the trends during those years are similar (see Figure A-1).[7] More investigation is needed to determine why the earnings recorded in the CWHS for that period were lower than those reported in the CPS. One possibility is that individuals with very low annual earnings tended to report that they had no earnings when responding to the CPS, in which case they would be excluded from that sample but would be found in the CWHS.

End Notes

[1]. CBO found patterns for men's and women's earnings in the CPS data that were similar to those found in the other data set used in this paper, the Continuous Work History Sample maintained by the Social Security Administration (see the appendix for more details).

[2]. CBO calculated the number of hours worked per year by multiplying the usual hours worked per week by the weeks worked per year.

[3]. See Joseph G. Altonji and Rebecca M. Blank, "Race and Gender in the Labor Market," in Orley Ashenfelter and David Card, eds., *Handbook of Labor Economics,* vol. 3C (New York: Elsevier, 1999), pp. 3143–3259.

[4]. For a discussion of changes in the bottom half of the hourly wage distribution, see Congressional Budget Office, *Changes in Low-Wage Labor Markets Between 1979 and 2005* (December 2006).

[5]. There were roughly 53 million men ages 25 to 54 working in 2005, so approximately 2.7 million of those men were in the top 5 percent of their earnings distribution. (Data were derived from a search of *Labor Force Statistics from the Current Population Survey,* Department of Labor, Bureau of Labor Statistics, September 23, 2009.)

[6]. According to one study, the share of earnings held by the top 1 percent of workers fell between 1937 and the mid-1960s before rising over the next 40 years. See Wojciech Kopczuk, Emmanuel Saez, and Jae Song, *Uncovering the American Dream: Inequality and Mobility in Social Security Earnings Data Since 1937,* Working Paper No. 13345 (Cambridge, Mass.: National Bureau of Economic Research, August 2007).

[7]. Roughly 45 million women ages 25 to 54 had earnings in 2005, and so about 2.3 million of those women were in the top 5 percent of their earnings distribution. (Data were derived from a search of *Labor Force Statistics from the Current Population Survey.*)

[8]. Although Table 4 and Table 5 (often called "transition matrices" or "transition tables") are useful for examining earnings mobility, they have some shortcomings. Movement from the 59th to the 61st percentile and movement from the 41st to the 79th percentile are both measured as a transition from the middle to the fourth quintile, despite the difference in the magnitude of the two shifts. Movement from the 41st to the 59th percentile is not

considered a transition; a person who makes such a move remains in the middle quintile. Transition tables also have an inherent asymmetry: Workers in the bottom quintile cannot move down any farther in the distribution, and workers in the top quintile cannot move any farther up.

9. As was the case between 2000 and 2005 (see Table 4 and Table 5), between 1990 and 1995 and between 1995 and 2000, the percentage of women changing quintiles was about 2 percentage points higher than the percentage of men making such a change.

10. CBO published similar results in a paper titled *Recent Trends in the Variability of Individual Earnings and Household Income*, in June 2008. As CBO did for that analysis, it defined the percentage change for this study as $((et - et\text{-}1)/((et + et\text{-}1)/2)*100)$, which allows years of zero earnings to appear in the calculation. See also Congressional Budget Office, "Trends in Earnings Variability Over the Past 20 Years," attachment to a letter to the Honorable Charles E. Schumer and the Honorable Jim Webb (April 17, 2007).

11. As noted in CBO's June 2008 publication on the variability of earnings, the results of that analysis are consistent with those in the economics literature, although explicit comparisons with other studies are complicated by differences in data and methodology.

12. In earlier work (see Congressional Budget Office, *The Role of Immigrants in the U.S. Labor Market*, November 2005), CBO concluded that "the arrival of large numbers of immigrants with little education probably slows the growth of the [hourly] wages of native-born high school dropouts, at least initially, but the ultimate impact on [hourly] wages is difficult to quantify." For a general description of the foreign-born population, see Congressional Budget Office, *A Description of the Immigrant Population* (November 2004).

13. See David H. Autor and Mark G. Duggan, "The Growth in the Social Security Disability Rolls: A Fiscal Crisis Unfolding," *Journal of Economic Perspectives*, vol. 20, no. 3 (Summer 2006), pp. 71–96.

14. See Table V.C5 in Social Security Administration, *The 2009 Annual Report of the Board of Trustees of the Federal Old-Age and Survivors Insurance and Federal Disability Insurance Trust Funds* (www.ssa.gov/OACT/TR/2009/lr5c5.html).

15. Personal communication to the Congressional Budget Office by staff members of the Department of Justice's Bureau of Justice Statistics, March 13, 2009.

16. The Census Bureau does not interview incarcerated individuals for the Current Population Survey. An increase in the percentage of people who were incarcerated would probably translate into an increase in the employment rate shown in Figure 10 because those who remained in the workforce would most likely have had a higher rate of employment than incarcerated individuals would have had if they had not been imprisoned. See Congressional Budget Office, *The Effect of Changes in Labor Markets on the Natural Rate of Unemployment* (April 2002).

17. The hourly wage discussed here is a calculated hourly wage (that is, annual earnings divided by the number of hours worked per year) rather than a reported hourly wage. As such, mismeasurement in the number of hours worked translates directly into mismeasurement in the hourly wage. See Nathaniel Baum-Snow and Derek Neal, "Mismeasurement of Usual Hours Worked in the Census and ACS," *Economics Letters,* vol. 102 (January 2009), pp. 39–41; and Greg J. Duncan and Daniel H. Hill, "An Investigation of the Extent and Consequences of Measurement Error in Labor-Economic Survey Data," *Journal of Labor Economics*, vol. 3, no. 4 (October 1985), pp. 508–532.

End Notes for Apendix

1. Workers are defined as people who have earnings of more than zero. However, the primary results of this paper are not sensitive to the exclusion of workers with very low annual earnings. For example, the basic conclusions remain unchanged if workers are defined as people who have earnings of more than $1,000.

2. See Marc I. Roemer, *Assessing the Quality of the March Current Population Survey and the Survey of Income and Program Participation Income Estimates, 1990–1996* (Bureau of the Census, Housing and Household Economic Statistics Division, Income Surveys Branch, June 16, 2000), www.census.gov/hhes/www/income/ assess1.pdf.

3. Details about those changes may be found in Bureau of the Census, *Current Population Survey, March 1995: Technical Documentation* (October 1995).

4. For discussions of the validity of survey reports of earnings compared with that of administrative records of earnings, see John M. Abowd and Martha H. Stinson, "Estimating Measurement Error in SIPP Annual Job Earnings: A Comparison of Census Survey and SSA Administrative Data" (draft, January 2005), http://courses.cit.cornell.edu/jma7/abowd-stinson-200501.pdf; John Bound and Alan B. Krueger, "The Extent of Measurement Error in Longitudinal Earnings Data: Do Two Wrongs Make a Right?" *Journal of Labor Economics,* vol. 9, no. 1 (January 1991), pp. 1–24; and Julian Cristia and Jonathan A. Schwabish, *Measurement Error in the SIPP: Evidence from Matched Administrative Records,* Congressional Budget Office Working Paper 2007-03 (January 2007).

5. See Table 1 in Mark A. Ledbetter, "Comparison of BEA Estimates of Personal Income and IRS Estimates of Adjusted Gross Income: New Estimates for 2004 and Revised Estimates for 2003," *Survey of Current Business,* vol. 86, no. 11 (Bureau of Economic Analysis, November 2006), pp. 29–36 6. House Committee on Ways and Means, *2004 Green Book: Background Material and Data on the Programs Within the Jurisdiction of the Committee on Ways and Means,* WMCP:108-6 (March 2004), Table 1-7 and p. 1-4.

7. For a comparison of earnings at the top of the distribution in the CPS and the CWHS, see Jonathan A. Schwabish, *Earnings Inequality and High Earners: Changes During and After the Stock Market Boom of the 1990s,* Congressional Budget Office Working Paper 2006-06 (April 2006).

INDEX